TOO

MUCH

BY

HALF

ISBN-13: 978 107 844 231 2

JAMES DIETRICH

TOO MUCH
BY HALF

THE COMING CUT

IN PROVED

OIL RESERVES

For Mary Keenan, Amy Allyson and Ida Sky

CONTENTS

PART THREE: WRITE-DOWN OF RESERVES

PREFACE

The year was 2007 and the financial world was crashing. The setting was my flat in Moscow, Russia. An American PhD economist working for the *Russell 2000 Index* asked me, "And how good are the estimates of proved oil reserves in *your* industry." She knew that mathematical models are used to predict value and risk in her world of money and in my world of oil. Perhaps she felt a sense of humiliation — the financial models had totally failed. I recall my response, "It seems that a barrel of oil reserves becomes three barrels if it's under Russia." That was a flip answer, but perhaps not that exaggerated. Her question stayed with me. Eight years later given even more international consulting experience, my sober answer became, "Proved oil reserves are too much by half." In other words, globally and on average, three barrels of publicized oil reserves are actually closer to two barrels.

Here we're talking only about proved reserves. These are hydrocarbon volumes that are estimated with reasonable certainty to be commercially recoverable. In probabilistic terms, use of the words *reasonable certainty* implies there is a 90% chance of meeting or exceeding the quoted recoverable volumes. Proved reserves represent a high-confidence estimate of the recoverable resources, one that is widely used by investors and bankers. And when the word *oil* is used, it's meant to apply to liquid crude oil in some cases and to natural gas, or gas condensate, in others, where equivalent amounts of energy are held in a "barrel" of each resource.

During periods of rising and falling oil prices, oil companies increase and decrease their estimates of proved reserves, in order to satisfy the requirement that the reserves are commercially recoverable. This is the story of how reserves have become systematically inflated, *aside* from any influence of rising oil prices. The book is part way between memoir and non-fiction — too much of one to be properly the other. Dubbed *narrative non-fiction*, it may appeal to those interested in the "peak oil" debate, an international consulting career, expat living, or simply the absurdity of people trying to work together.

My views on the reserves question are derived from working independently for decades inside Big Oil. They are likely to differ from the perceptions of outsiders who rely on material made available for public consumption. Consider the attorney working as a financial services executive who has written a book about oil in 2016. He tells us we're at the dawn of the fossil fuel era, touting that his book "... incorporates *facts* from leading authorities and firsthand sources, such as the revenue *predictions* of major oil companies and the United States government." Since when are we expected to accept an equivalence between *facts* and *predictions*?

The technology used to predict reserves goes by several different names: either reservoir modeling, mathematical modeling or reservoir simulation. This book describes the emergence of this powerful technology and the role of the author in it, beginning at Shell Development (R&D) Company. At the heart of the narrative is the struggle between reservoir engineers and geologists for control of the modeling process. That power play has now reached an end with success going to the earth scientists. "How does the title *Too Much by Half* relate to a power play?" The rules of the game have quietly been changed by the new masters. During the prior reign of engineering, oil trapped in poor quality rock was excluded from reserves. That oil was known to be present, but it was cut-out of the models because it could not be made to flow. It was not considered to be a portion of proven reserves. That was the status for decades. Under the new dominion of earth science, oil stored in poor quality rock is entered into the reservoir models and made accessible by combining it with the better quality rock. I call this process *Moonbeam Modeling.* It's like making high risk junk bonds accessible to investors by combining them with bonds rated AAA to A and marketing the lot as bonds rated BBB to B — still good enough to attract capital. The difficult to move junk bonds and inaccessible oil can be made to "flow" by fictitiously upgrading them.

Why write a book about excess and over-optimism? After all, it's normal for the owner of an asset to over-value it. However, in the case of oil, it's more than about greed and the need to attract capital — there's that important topic of "peak oil". In 2010, "James Schlesinger, the former head of the CIA and the Pentagon for whom Jimmy Carter had created the U.S. secretary of energy office, stated that the debate on peak oil was over, and the 'peakists have won'". And then came the shale oil revolution in the United States, renewing claims that the world is awash in oil, claims uttered once again by oil industry outsiders who think they're *in the know.* What's often considered *shale oil* is actually oil held in better quality rock called *siltstone,* the same type of rock that has been exploited for decades in many parts of the world using hydraulic fracturing technology. Both are of poor quality, but when given the choice between developing shale or siltstone, the siltstone is like low-hanging fruit — it's taken (or drilled) first. Production from poor quality rocks is known to decline rapidly. And it's common for a new well to temporarily accelerate overall production from a reservoir by *stealing* oil from older, neighboring wells. In this situation, frenzied drilling and fracking brought on by increased oil prices will increase oil rate and cash flow, but only temporarily. Therefore, it's no surprise for those really *in the know* to read, "90% of American shale operators had a negative cash flow even when crude prices were higher."

Shale oil is only one of several resources that are collectively labeled *extreme petroleum.* It's said that in Colorado, Wyoming and Utah there is more shale oil than all the conventional oil in the world. However, "Shale oil in the ground is not oil at all — it was so named in order to attract investment." It is kerogen, organic matter that can be made into oil if the rock containing it is mined, crushed and heated, in a process that is not presently commercial. There is no shale oil revolution — it's a *siltstone oil revolution*, one that is likely to be short-lived.

The book was written to counter the claims that we are awash in oil. A term called the R/P ratio is central to the debate on peak oil. It's the ratio of known reserves to the rate of use — the ratio is about 40 years for oil and 60 years for natural gas. If world reserves are indeed over-booked by half, those estimates shorten to nearly 25 years for oil and 40 years for gas. We will likely have a lot less time to move away from the use of fossil fuels before the tanks are empty. And then consider: The worldwide supply of oil, as of any mineral resource, will rise from zero to a peak and after that will decline forever. The crisis comes not when the last drop is pumped; it arrives when we've consumed nearly half the oil there ever was. At that point, steadily falling supply can not meet continuing rising demand. Nearly all the pundits agree that we're close to the half-way point.

The book reads mostly as memoir, telling the story as a chronology of projects in which the author was retained as a consultant to develop and produce reserves. The reader will get the sense that as we're reaching the half-way point, it's nature — geology and fluid mechanics — that is preventing us from unlocking more oil from old reservoirs, never mind oil prices!

Part One

The Reign
of Engineering

CHAPTER ONE

THE HOOK WAS SET

It was the year 1962 and I was 20. Unlike many young people of that era, I was neither a product of the 60's, nor a rebel without a clue. As half a Teuton, I seemed to like order and structure. I was a sophomore at the University of California in Santa Barbara and, although serious and hard-working, I was on academic probation. I first understood the reason for this to be a poor preparation in high school math and science that left me struggling to catch up with the competition in my chosen field of physical science. However, later it became clear that it was more about an inability to handle distraction. I was unable to party with my peers and then flip the switch to focus on class work — a classic sign of immaturity.

During the probationary times, my parents were overheard to say, "Our poor young son, he and his two older siblings are like chalk and cheese." One of these perfect siblings had been the homecoming queen in high school, had her own radio station at age 16, had been introduced to society as a debutante and, at the time, was the president of her sorority while on a full academic ride at the University of Southern California. The other a brother, who had been born one of those "old souls" and who was gifted, probably from conception. He had been offered an appointment at the U.S. Naval Academy, receiving one of the two entrance recommendations made each year by the California state governor. Failing to meet the minimum vision requirements, he was rejected by the Navy and was devastated. Lo, he was forced to accept his second choice, a combined academic and athletic football scholarship offered by Stanford University.

What to do? I had seen a few friends dropout and enter the military, but this seemed a dire course. Surely, even for this loser, it was too early for that! The summer was approaching and I knew it would be a tough slog to return to my parents' home after leaving them at age 17. It was my brother, now employed as a petroleum engineer with the Continental Oil Company (Conoco) in Ponca City, Oklahoma, who without knowing provided the model that led me through the next critical months. Upon finishing the school year, I drove to Ojai, California, to begin looking for a summer job in the oil industry. Why the oil industry is obvious. Why Ojai? Well, it was a scenic little town and very near Santa Paula, where the Union Oil Corporation was founded. More importantly, it was where the actor Steve McQueen had a residence and stabled his fast cars and motorcycles in a hanger at the general aviation airport. If the king of cool had chosen that place, it would be good enough for me.

I was clueless that morning in June 1962, without even a hint that Rocky Mountain Drilling Company would soon become my employer. While driving from the coastal town of Ventura towards Ojai on Hwy 33, I noticed their sign along the road in the little town of Oak View. I stopped, walked into the office and up to a man seated at a desk. He was Dorsey Stratis, president of the company. I extended my hand and introduced myself as a geology student on probation at the University of California, knowing that a revealed lack of academic prowess would probably not lose me the job. I said I would like to roughneck for the summer while sorting out my future. I recall he gave me an amused look before agreeing to take me on, with the caveat that I would first need to steam-clean oilfield equipment in the yard for a period of two weeks. I started several days later after renting a little house in Oak View, verbally assuring the landlord that Rocky Mountain Drilling would be paying me $2.90/hour. That pay rate was standard in the industry and equivalent to much more than the salary of a college graduate working in areas other than science and engineering. Finding a job in those days was all so simple and straightforward! I recall the rental was a very small wooden structure, painted a barn-red, located along side the highway and, of course, without air conditioning. It proved to be a perfect accommodation for a young guy on his own, the type of place where a king snake stuck one night in maple syrup that had dripped onto the linoleum kitchen floor could simply be ignored until it could be freed the next day upon return from work. The landlord's place was not far up the dirt road around a hill. His young wife was a stunner, a figure who would frequently be imagined as other than unavailable during the long, hot summer.

Rocky Mountain Drilling Company was moving in a rig to re-drill a 17,000-ft well on the Ventura Anticline. Thinking it was a necessary initiation test to pass, I had gladly accepted the role of steam cleaner, knowing the work would involve removing congealed oil from steel outside and without cover, when the daily temperatures would be exceeding 105 degrees. Now I learned that the roughnecking work would not be able to start until the rig was on location. The steam cleaning was just a way to get me signed up and on payroll prior the start of the real work. Dorsey Stratis must have taken a liking to me!

To this day I don't know how it happened. As part of the yard work, I was asked to help with cutting drill pipe that would be used to demarcate parking spaces in a parking lot. A cut section of pipe fell on and flattened my left big toe. Had I been wearing steel-capped boots which I could not afford, probably more damage would have been done. In that case, the steel cap may have severed multiple toes. I remained silent when this happened. I thought to say nothing was to keep the job, and that was probably the right decision.

I found a doctor after hours who prescribed medication for pain relief and saved the toe.

A well depth of 17,000 feet was pretty deep in those days. When approaching the drill site at the beginning of a work shift, the derrick where the drill pipe was racked could be seen at a distance of a mile or two, as one wound along the switch-back dirt lease roads. This was of keen interest because whether the drill pipe was being entered into the hole or being pulled from it could be determined from viewing the movement of the traveling blocks and the amount of pipe standing in the pipe rack. If the crew were just coming out of the hole, this meant that a tough shift was in store, for it would take most of the 8-hour shift to pull the pipe, replace the drill bit on the end of it, and then run in the hole again to resume drilling at bottom depth. One wanted to avoid round tripping whenever possible.

A pressing need that summer was to get along with the other roughnecks, all from very different backgrounds than mine and many of whom were native Americans from Oklahoma. That I had even heard of Ponca City was a plus, but not much of one. Using seed money gifted from my father a few years earlier for the purchase of my first automobile, I had traded up to a 1956 Porsche Speedster for a sum of $1,400, getting a good deal from a member of the U.S. Marine Corps who was one of the earliest being deployed to Vietnam. It was bright red in color and a convertible, a classic that today is worth $400,000. Its 1600cc engine could push it along at a top speed of only 100 mph, but boy how it could handle. As the new temporary hire, my shift was of course from midnight to 0800 hours. Imagine showing up at the drilling rig with this ride, even in the dark. I recall trying to hide it from view. When changing in the doghouse preparing for work, the comments began coming my way. Even my close inspection of the girly magazine-cutouts on the doghouse walls failed to improve my welcome. I said that as half a Teuton it was the German engineering that caused me to choose this type of ride. I knew that response was lost on the doghouse crowd when a native American said the little car could not possibly be that heavy.

That night we were round tripping for the entire shift, with only quick breaks for peeing possible between the pulling of 90-foot sections of pipe. Earth stresses were high within the Ventura Anticline and an unusual amount of pipe stress had developed while drilling the highly deviated wellbore. The rocks were so heavily folded and faulted that they were upside down. In some places, the drill bit would actually penetrate the bottom, or older part, of a stratum first before reaching its top. The men from Oklahoma had not previously encountered such stresses in the stable, central part of the country, where the forces of plate tectonics were absent. When we broke the pipe joints, energy released from breaking the joints caused the freed pipe sections to bounce wildly around within the derrick. This went on for hours. I thought this was normal, all others knew it was not. Eyes were wide and a few hard hats were knocked off, including mine, but no one required an ambulance ride that long night. Because I was too inexperienced to be alarmed, it seemed to others that I was fearless. Basically they were just clueless that I was clueless. When on bottom making hole, there is no pipe to pull and a seasoned roughneck will take the opportunity to hide and stretch out somewhere on the rig floor, especially during a night shift. Imagine their surprise when awakened by some drip running around with an oil can in his hand acting like the fine print of his employment contract had true meaning. They must have thought Custer and the cavalry were coming. I quickly learned to avoid oiling anything near the warm sleeping areas beneath the big Waukesha compressors.

The college kid was accepted and summer passed quickly. I was smart enough not to make a move on the landlord's wife. I think it was out of principle, but I am not sure. Perhaps I was just bone tired from round tripping with very few days off. With two weeks left before the start of my third school year, the re-drilled well from hell was complete. My last duties involved help with taking down the derrick and readying the rig for a move to the next location. An offer for continued employment was made. I declined, appreciating that I still had all my fingers and all but one of my toes.

I had to improve my grade point average to a C level upon my return to campus for the fall semester. The cost of failure was expulsion from academia, likely followed I thought by entry into the military as a grunt or into the oil fields as a roughneck. What a predictable ending for the black sheep of the family! I liked my chosen major in geology in a Bachelor of Arts program that required a number of courses in the humanities for graduation. Unfortunately, my aptitude seemed to be higher for subjects other than science and math. The good news was that I had memorized the textbook required for a French language course and was consistently receiving the highest possible test scores in that subject, bar none. There was a glimmer of hope, although I knew that pursuit of a degree in humanities was definitely not for me.

There were ten of us in the geology class of 1964. Two had been in the military and were older. They were smart, focused and definitely not clueless. Another classmate became my roommate. As the son of two college professors, he was a natural academic and the one who walked off with more than one scholastic award bestowing financial assistance. Then there was a mystery man who would appear for some classes of any given course, but not for others. He would join some required field trips but not all of them. He was a good looking, athletic, very bright guy who was a member of the Sigma Alpha Epsilon fraternity and very well liked by both men and women. This enigmatic classmate was taking and skipping classes for credit or simply auditing them, in either case it must have been with special approval from the Dean of Students. It came as no surprise when I learned years later that this prior classmate was the Robert Ballard. This the man who went on to get his doctorate in geophysics, later reaching the pinnacle of his field in oceanography with discovery of the seafloor wreckage of the RMS Titanic, the German battleship Bismarck and the U.S.S. Yorktown. And finally of special mention was the only female in the class. Competent in her own right, her academic standing must have been further elevated when she and a new assistant professor of geology became an item. With this kind of class profile, no wonder I was finding it hard to compete for grades in physical science!

That fall term, I returned home for the Thanksgiving break. We were a secular family, never before asking God for his blessings at meal time or, in fact, at any other time. It was therefore surprising when my father began the meal with a prayer. Surely all six of the other family members present that day were also amazed. All was clarified when he asked the Lord for divine intervention on behalf of his son, the dunce. This irritated me greatly. I abruptly left the table and was on the road back to school before dessert was served. It was harsh yet right in style for my father, the full Teuton. The prayer for help did the trick. Henceforth from the missed thanksgiving dinner until graduation a few years later in 1964, nearly all A-level grades fell my way.

The final requirement for graduation was completion of a geology field mapping course of duration six weeks. The location was Santa Cruz Island, 25 miles off the coast of Santa Barbara. A fault splits the island into two halves, uplifting and exposing volcanic rocks on the north and older sedimentary rocks on the south; it was the perfect place for looking at rocks. Our class was the first allowed on the privately owned island, where cattle ranching had been in progress for decades. We set up camp with sleeping areas uncovered and open to the sky. The stars were usually countless in number, clearly visible in the absence of light pollution. It was an awkward start when the only female in the class had to be evacuated by helicopter to the mainland for treatment of bride's disease, suffered as a result of saying, "I do," to the assistant professor a few days before traveling to the island. When the island owner was required to make a rare overnight trip to the mainland for an unknown but surely different reason, I was asked by our head professor to make myself present for the evening at the main ranch house. I was puzzled at the purpose and not told of it. The time of my arrival had been set close to the cocktail hour. As no alcohol and no women were stipulations for our allowed island invasion, I was sensing that after a month now the dry spell would soon be ending for me. I just knew that a beer or more would likely be on offer, never mind hope upon hope for the possibility of female company. Indeed I shared a scotch whiskey or two that evening with a man who is truly one of those unforgettable people in life. He was the boss of about twenty Mexican vaqueros who were billeted on the island and responsible for cattle management. There was no law on the island at that time as it was not a territory of the United States or any other country. His holstered six gun was resting on a dresser next to the scotch bottle. It was more than a showpiece, for later it was learned that he had recently used it to detain and jail a horny vaquero who had insisted on getting more than a meal from the female cook, before returning him to Mexico. Why does this qualify the man as unforgettable? It's because he was a paraplegic. Without the use of his legs, he drove a specially outfitted jeep and served as the only law on the island. I had been chosen that evening to fill-in for the absent island owner. My job was to pick the man up, help him into his pajamas and put him in bed after we quaffed enough scotch to make it all go smoothly. I enjoyed meeting the boss with no legs and felt privileged to have been selected for the cause.

Each classmate was of legal age and each was required to sign a document stating that the beauty of the island would not be made public via any means. Upon the death of the private owner in 1987, most of the real property passed per prior agreement to The Nature Conservancy, an environmental non-profit organization. The remainder of the island belongs to the National Park Service. It is truly a stunning place. One can almost see through the breaking waves that are more than translucent. Successful completion of that mapping course was a perfect way to end the academic program. Now, with a Bachelor of Arts degree in-hand, I felt like more than a dunce.

During my last academic year, it had become clear that rocks alone were not going to be enough for me. Two of us in the geology program were sharing a house with two other men, one majoring in pre-law and the other in pre-med. While neither law nor medicine itself was of interest, the life styles of these two guys were appealing. They were having fun! When the other geology major and I would head out each Saturday morning before dawn for a required field mapping class, we drove past the fraternities and sororities where all night partying was just entering its final stages. Then, upon our return, when sunburned and weary, and after duly describing rocks laid out on the kitchen table, it would be necessary to separate various pieces of lingerie from our bedding before getting to sleep. Our roommates enjoyed themselves in our absence, knowing there was more to life than playing with rocks. It was after all California, the 1960's and the wild campus bedroom community of Isla Vista. My hunch was that few, if any, of these party animals were majoring in STEM (science, technology, engineering and math) subjects.

I knew I had little aptitude for a career in STEM, yet this acronym defined my areas of interest. How boring and therefore hopeless it would have been to consider an easier road more frequently traveled. With my newfound confidence in academics, I began to consider various topics for graduate school. Although more geology was definitely in the mix, there was too much science in it alone. Too much was open to interpretation. At that time, something called the Theory of Isostasy was a fundamental geological concept taught everywhere in universities of the world. It called on buoyancy forces to explain mountain building and that seemed absurd to me and other classmates. Based on little more than conjecture, that theory was later replaced by an understanding of plate tectonics, a subject which had not even been introduced to the class of 1964. Our physical science textbooks ridiculed the concept of plate tectonics and a student at that time had to give the wrong answer to get an A grade. Proving to be much more than a finder of shipwrecks, our classmate Robert Ballard would later advance physical science by shrinking the need for teaching absurdity. He did this by filming the process of seafloor spreading from a submersible robot positioned near the deep ocean floor. His images showing movement of tectonic plates in real time really could be described as earth shaking! Most scientists considered them to mark a quick death for the Theory of Isostasy.

I wanted something more quantitative than geology, notwithstanding my earlier need for private tutoring in high school algebra and an inability to earn other than poor grades in college physics and calculus. In fact, the quantitative academic courses were the very ones that had placed me on probation. When attending a private luncheon in Santa Barbara during my last academic year, I became aware of a career choice that seemed perfect. I met men there who were partners in a small, privately owned, civil engineering consulting firm. The owners were only four in number. They were without bosses, answerable only to their clients, obviously financially comfortable and, best of all, STEM guys!

The professor who had negotiated the terms and logistics for the invasion of Santa Cruz Island (Donald Weaver) was a recently retained consultant to Dames & Moore, Inc., a civil engineering firm in Los Angeles. Their projects included the building of tunnels, dams and underground hydro-electric power stations. They were expanding into hydrology and soil mechanics and hiring graduates from the emerging career fields of engineering geology and geotechnical engineering. My long term goal was now clear: it was to become bossless, like the Santa Barbara consultants. Somehow, combining engineering and geology was going to be my way forward to secure the goal.

As if the scotch drunk at the ranch house was not reward enough, the same professor who had made that possible set up an interview for me with his client Dames & Moore, when I said his consulting work sounded interesting. During that interview, I was offered a junior position with my BA degree in geology. However, at the same time a written offer was given which stipulated that a much higher paying staff position would be mine upon completion of a MS degree in engineering science from U.C. Berkeley. A number of courses were specified that needed to be a part of the curriculum, all completed with an overall grade point average of B, or better. I had applied for graduate school admission to Purdue University and the University of Alberta, Edmonton. When Purdue rejected me, I applied to Berkeley, given encouragement by Professor Weaver, understanding that its graduate program in Civil Engineering was ranked first in the nation and was among the best in the world. Its MS program requires two years for completion, a good thing in my case because time was needed to make up undergraduate physical science courses missing from my program.

U.C. Berkeley must have agreed to take me after being astonished that one with such a slow start could turn it all around so quickly. Lo and behold the power of a thanksgiving prayer. More likely, my acceptance was due to the pull of Professor Weaver, who had received his PhD from Berkeley in 1959. I enrolled there in the Department of Civil Engineering in the fall of 1964 and graduated with a MS in the summer of 1966, completing the very same curriculum specified by Dames & Moore. My overall grade point average of 3.6/4.0 was much higher than a B, so all was good. My thesis advisor was a brilliant, very young assistant professor, who had received his PhD only months earlier. Richard Goodman would quickly become a full professor and eventually be elected to the U.S. National Academy of Engineering, the highest distinction awarded to an engineer. He is a world class expert in rock mechanics, a consultant in demand by clients throughout the world and presently an Emeritus Professor of Engineering. He would hop on a plane and fly to Italy for evaluation of what went wrong when an earthen dam failed, or advise the way forward when a tunnel-boring machine became stuck in Switzerland. Income received from this activity must have exceeded what he earned as a professor. It was later understood that this model of an international consulting life style would heavily influence my own career choices. Goodman secured a research assistantship for me, a position partly funded by the Pacific Gas & Electric (PG&E) company. I was paid for 20 hours each week, testing the strength of rock samples in a massive hydraulic press in the Hearst Memorial Mining Building, a granite edifice that looks like a European manor house on the Berkeley campus. Some rocks failed suddenly, releasing so much energy that the noise would deafen and the granite building would seem to shake, hoped at the time to unsettle those majoring in humanities in adjacent buildings who were reading Descartes while sipping lattes and planning their next anti-war demonstration with Jane Fonda.

My thesis involved field mapping and a solo overnight trip to the Tuolumne River running through the Yosemite National Park. On the honor system, I was to speak with no one while in the field for 36 hours evaluating bedrock that would become the foundation of the New Don Pedro Dam, which began construction the next year. I didn't need much honor to play by the rules, for my written instructions put me in an abandoned mining shack the size of a big outhouse, with no electricity, no phones and no humans for miles. It was a long, dark, uncomfortable night filled with the distant sounds of yapping coyotes and the close sounds of a black bear. There were several adits at the site, which are horizontal passages leading into a mine. I entered two of the three to look at the exposed bedrock. A Northern Pacific rattle snake was coiled and rattling at the narrow opening of the third adit, which I chose not to enter. As a result, I missed some small faults in the bedrock that were a key part of the site description. When asked about this omission from Professor Goodman, I replied, "I would have had to kill a rattle snake to enter that adit." Good thing Goodman was ecological, for a report describing my field work was accepted, marking a winning end to my academic life. Not bad, field work on beautiful Santa Cruz Island for a BA degree and more field work in magnificent Yosemite National Park for a MS degree.

My military draft status was 1-A in 1966, meaning that I was callable for active duty at any time. The call had not come in yet, because I was enrolled full-time in an accredited academic program in good standing. In an exaggerated sense of power, one of my math professors had let me know how he personally had spared me from peril, by rounding a final grade up rather than down to keep me in good standing. He must have felt it was his contribution to the war effort. Although my views on the Vietnam war were negative, I did not join the many anti-war demonstrations while in graduate school. The engineering course work was grueling. I was fully committed to the program, and it seemed unlikely that the military industrial complex and our politicians were going to be slowed by public protest. The options of conscientious objection, immigrating to Canada or voluntary gender change were not for me. As graduation neared, a letter from the draft board could arrive any day. My plan was to volunteer as a candidate in an officer training program, preferably in the U.S. Navy, to avoid being inducted as an Army infantryman. I had been interested in submarines since reading Run Silent, Run Deep as a teenager and thought being underwater would be a good way to escape the jungles of Vietnam. A month prior to graduation, I made an appointment with a Navy recruiter at the Federal Building in San Francisco. When I learned there were no openings in a Navy officer training program, I walked down the hall to talk with a U.S. Marine Corps recruiter, who quickly had me taking a written qualification exam and repeatedly pronouncing the motto "Semper Fidelis." They scored the test and passed me, ignoring that I did not know the difference between a bull and a bear financial market. I was to return two weeks later to enter Officer Candidates School after passing a medical exam and signing the induction papers. The eventual slot of a platoon leader with the rank of 2nd Lieutenant and the probable life span of only a few months had my name on it.

My brother telephoned a few days later. He would soon be on the Berkeley campus, interviewing students who were graduating and interested in employment with Conoco. The timing must have been purely coincidental, for he would have had interviews scheduled well in advance on his multi-university recruiting trip. When we met for dinner the night of his arrival, he described federal legislation that offered a critical skills deferment from military service for engineers employed in the oil industry. He was sharp on the subject, having been schooled on it by the Conoco HR Department in preparation for his campus visits. The concept was that petroleum engineers were needed at home to ensure the continuing supply of fuel for planes and ships. Dames & Moore had only laid out an academic plan for me, they had not funded it. There were no obligations.

I interviewed several energy companies and upon graduation received job offers from Mobil, Shell Oil Company and Schlumberger Ltd. Schlumberger offered an opportunity to make a lot of money quickly, as a field engineer driving a service truck from one oil well to another in various parts of the world. It would be intense field work, with very long hours. It was rumored that burnout would be rapid. I passed on that offer. I had no student debt, thanks in part to my research assistantship — money was not my primary interest. At the time, Shell Oil was a subsidiary of Royal Dutch Shell of the Netherlands. It is an American company, headquartered in Houston, with little likelihood for future overseas assignment. I signed with them in spite of this and their offer of $775/month, which was the lowest of all. Their technical training schools were tops, arguably approached only by those of Chevron and Exxon, and they were packed with the top names in research and development. I asked for and received their commitment to employ me as a petroleum engineer, not as a geologist.

I had never known either of my grandfathers, nor had I been aware of their business interests at the time of my matriculation. My maternal grandfather had owned and operated what was termed a silica mine in the public records near Cahuilla Mountain, not far from the town of Anza, inland from San Diego in California. He was actually mining for precious metals, not silica, and he died of silicosis of the lungs as a result of this activity. I was to learn years later that my paternal grandfather had worked as a roughneck for Shell Oil Company from 1923 to 1928 in the Wilmington oil field of California. It's uncanny that I chose geology as a major, was employed as a roughneck and chose Shell Oil Company as an employer, all in keeping with the unknown interests of my ancestors. Perhaps there really is something in the ether that connects everything.

CHAPTER TWO

PAYING MY DUES

A sense of dishonor is too strong to describe the emotion I felt upon signing with Big Oil. But something was not quite right. It was my emotion alone, not shared, as my classmates at Berkeley were nearly all foreign students who were not facing a military draft and the question of a career choice compromise. During an orientation meeting for new hires at Shell, two engineers from other American universities withdrew from their employment contracts. One announced he was going to accept an offer for employment as a social worker in Los Angeles, the other was leaving to make a pot-full of money selling something new called mutual funds. I realized at the moment that my unease had a different source, it had nothing to do with altruism or greed.

What my only uncle thought of me was important. He owned Merchants Fire Dispatch, a private security business inherited from his father, located in a tough downtown neighborhood of Los Angeles. His office building had been an interesting place to visit for his young nephew. It held a shooting range in the basement where the security guards practiced with their handguns. Equally attracting was a locker room where the guards exchanged their street clothing for uniforms with security badges. Later it was learned that the locker room walls displayed a more hard core collection of girly magazine cutouts than could be seen in the doghouses of Rocky Mountain Drilling Company. I liked him for reasons other than allowing me to view girly pictures. I recall not feeling thrilled when I shared the news of my employment with him. It was known then that I had settled for something less than my goal of working without a boss in a small consulting firm. It was nothing like what had been shared with him during his last visit in Berkeley, when we talked in our beds at the Jack London Inn in neighboring Oakland, with lights out like young kids.

Shell handled the paperwork needed to secure my critical skills deferment from military service. I remained with them for 10-½ years and now enjoy a small monthly pension, which covers the recurring cost of cabernet sauvignon that is usually too young to drink. The training schools were of high caliber. They were given at the Bellaire Research Center of Shell Development Company in Houston, and typically the instructors held PhD degrees. Top company executives and senior managers were invariably drawn from the Exploration and Production (E&P) Department, where I worked, and they were home grown. All were STEM men. Those holding the top technical titles were paid as much as vice presidents. It was truly a meritocracy!

I left the company during my third year, only for a short time as it turned out. The siren's song was calling, the lure of working without a boss in a small consulting firm was far too great. Although not clear at the time, I was looking for a reason to leave. The trigger that set the timing of my departure was a difference of opinion with management about the volumes of oil and gas reserves recoverable from key leases in the Coalinga oil field of California. The push by management of all companies to inflate reserve estimates is the main subject of this book. It was a problem that would persist throughout my career, regardless of whether it was a number for a single well, a lease, or an entire oil field. A STEM man was responsible for calculating a reserve estimate and supporting it whenever it was audited, using technical principles and a self-consistent set of assumptions. Never mind how the world works, it all had to fit together! How could an owner or manager with a bias for high numbers be allowed to intervene in the reserve reporting process? With no job prospect in mind, I submitted a letter of resignation, sold my house and moved to San Francisco, all within a week and with an earnest sense of indignation. The credentials from U.C. Berkeley allowed me to promptly secure a consulting engineering position with the small firm of Harding, Miller, Lawson & Associates, specializing in soil mechanics and geotechnical engineering.

I quickly learned that combining engineering and geology in a civil engineering firm was not going to be my path to career happiness, after all. It was annoying that the work schedule was unpredictable and strongly controlled by weather and traffic. The customer location and nature of the job on any given day usually became known only hours in advance, not good for someone who liked predictability. It rained a lot in the Bay Area, and when it did, work was commonly stopped. I missed routine and structure. Moreover, several completed projects had provided nowhere near the excitement of the oil patch, although the last of them came close. That one involved rescuing the Lawrence Berkeley National Laboratory from the threat of a landslide. Its offices housed a number of the nation's top scientists, who looked out through walls of glass at stunning green hills behind the Berkeley campus. One of the hills was slowly moving toward this mass of brainpower. It was time to stop it before the onset of the rainy season when its movement was sure to accelerate. It was my project. Each day a D8 Caterpillar would roar to life early in the morning and its operator would cut out the upper part of the hill that was creeping down slope on a slide plane, moving and spreading it out in a series of thin layers in front of the office walls of glass. It was just the unfriendly ex-con driving the bull dozer and myself on-site each day. We rarely spoke — give me a native American at Rocky Mountain Drilling any day! By regulatory code, each layer of soil needed to be rolled and compacted to an acceptable density before the next layer could be spread on top of it. While on my knees performing the density tests with my little kit, the operator would inch up to me with all 650 hp of his D8 snarling at my butt in a type of standoff later exemplified, with a 180-degree twist, at Tiananmen Square. A failed test would mean lost time for the earth moving company, for then it became necessary to add moisture to the soil and re-compact it before proceeding. As the protector of the code requirements, it was not possible for me to lose one of these standoffs. A failed test would bring on wild arm waving and strong argument, in full view of the Nobel laureates behind the walls of glass. I was stunned to view a hoard of them standing and silently applauding my efforts on my last day at Harding, Miller, Lawson & Associates.

The welcome back to Shell was a pleasant surprise. It had been a four-month hiatus. I returned to the Bakersfield office where I had left, focusing quickly and reporting to a new supervisor who was arriving from Houston. Filled with leadership qualities, Jack Little had played football and earned a PhD in petroleum engineering from Texas A&M University. He had the appearance of a golden boy, with teeth that were almost too white before the age of whitening strips was upon us. He set me up with a novel project and guided me through it. We published its results in a technical paper that marked my first publication and his last. He was moving up so fast that he had no time for such things as technical publications. Jack Little was good and I was glad to be back. He later became the president of Shell Oil Company and was inducted into the U.S. National Academy of Engineering. The paper was given at a conference in San Antonio, Texas, where my father had flown in as a surprise. Unlike today, the questions at the microphone following a technical presentation in those years could be absolutely brutal. Fortunately, there were few difficult questions and I was spared of embarrassment. The Americans led the world in petroleum engineering technology and our annual technical conference organized by the Society of Petroleum Engineers (SPE) became a venue where nationalism regularly reared its ugly head. The French were especially difficult.

Numerical reservoir simulation is a key technology that is presently a billion dollar per year space within the petroleum industry. The first commercially available reservoir simulator appeared in 1967, when an entrepreneur programmed something called the McCord simulator, based on knowledge presented at Stanford University's Computer Conference in 1964, the year of my graduation from U.C. Santa Barbara. The lifted knowledge had its roots in research undertaken by Chevron's California Research Corporation and Esso's Production Research Laboratory, both sponsored by Aramco, owned at the time by Exxon, Mobil, Chevron and Texaco. Reservoir simulation involves building a mathematical model of a reservoir and processing it on a computer to evaluate the oil recovery potential of alternative depletion schemes. A field development plan prepared today nearly always has its roots in reservoir simulation. Moreover, the value of a petroleum company is based on the volume of its reserves, which in turn are estimated using reservoir simulation. Prior to the breakthrough development of the mathematics and software programs at the heart of the technology, researchers built scaled physical models of oil fields and peered inside them through transparent surfaces to view the results of alternative depletion schemes. Physical models required years to build and they were expensive.

A chance to ride the new technology wave came in 1970, when Shell began moving from physical to numerical modeling. At that time, there were few applications of numerical simulation within the industry. There were hardly any company staff who had a background in both engineering and geology, the two major disciplines called for in the technology. Perhaps it was for this reason that the first major reservoir simulation project in Shell was assigned to me. Working with guidance from company research staff and in near isolation, I needed two full years to build a numerical model of the Middle Ground Shoal field in Alaska.

It was not uncommon for an employee to be transferred from operations to research and then back again, in a round trip covering a period of two years.

Toward the end of my career with Shell, a shift had taken place. The round trips were mostly being taken by PhDs from research to operations and then back to research, and in some cases there was no return at all. Competition was fierce for the management positions in the operating company. Those who hired into the operating company and were looking forward to moving up learned that the key slots often went to the doctorates from research. This survival of the fittest was not an issue for me. I wanted to be a STEM man, not a manager.

My boss in the Mathematical Modeling and Thermal Oil Recovery Group was the best possible mentor. His name is Bill Miller, an intellectual, reserved, highly professional and a Stanford graduate. With just a few words he could get the juices flowing and turn on light bulbs. He taught me how to look deep inside the source code and understand the engine that powered a numerical simulator. I did well and gained confidence under his guidance. I was promoted to a division reservoir engineer and returned to the operating company after two years. There were ten employees in my group: seven engineers, including two PhDs from the research company, and three technicians. One of our projects involved installing and operating a field pilot test of an enhanced oil recovery (EOR) process designed by Shell Development Company. The Coalinga Polymer Demonstration Project involved stirring polymer and water together in big mixing tanks on the surface before injecting the concoction into a reservoir to improve oil recovery. The process is called polymer flooding and it was so novel at the time that funds were available from the U.S. Energy Research and Development Administration (ERDA) for demonstrating its viability in a field pilot test. Major problems were occurring and the project was off schedule and over budget. Air had seeped into the wellheads to degrade the quality of the polymer, reducing the viscosity of the mixture to an ineffective level. The solution was to replace the standard wellheads with air-tight versions at very high cost. I recall traveling to Bartlesville, Oklahoma, with the top reservoir engineer in Shell Oil

Company (Todd Doscher), where I made the pitch for public funds during a presentation filled with heart palpitations, sourced from nervousness and too much caffeine. It was a big moment. In hindsight, it was a sure thing. My emotions given success could not even be described as mixed — they were negative. Why should Shell Oil Company take taxpayer funds given the requirement that all of its polymer flooding research be made public? In 1977, ERDA was combined with the Federal Energy Agency to form the U.S. Department of Energy, an organization that would resurface throughout my career as a major business annoyance.

The concoction was injected and very little oil came out. We knew during the first year, after consuming many man-years of research and planning, that failure was upon us. The reservoir had been described with closed boundaries for numerical simulation purposes, when in fact its edges were wide open. The injected concoction had simply run sideways out of the reservoir instead of sweeping oil out of it. A bunch of very bright men had failed, arguably because none of them had a practical background in both engineering and geology that would have allowed them to see the reservoir for what it was, and what it needed to be. Not surprisingly, there was no single point of accountability for this mess. Outsourcing the project to the right small consulting firm would have saved the company shareholders and public taxpayers a lot of money. It was this event that first brought to mind a rhetorical question that would go unvoiced many times for years to come, "How many people can an oil field support?"

The pace of work was too slow for me. The drip with the oil can in his hand at Rocky Mountain Drilling reappeared to knock on office doors closed too long for lunchtime bridge games, silently yelling, "Let's go!" After passing the date when a vested interest in my pension was earned, I began looking for the right time to again leave the big company. There were two triggers this time, one occurring only weeks before the other. The first was the plight of a young female technician, who asked to see me behind my closed office door.

Upon entering, she turned her back to me, pulled up her blouse, showed me whip marks on her skin and asked for help with intercepting her husband, who was on his way to do her further damage. Realizing it was best not to ask if foreplay had gotten out of hand, I remained silent and called security. What a distraction, a waste of time from something completely out of my control! There was no question that management was not for me. The second trigger was a demand to lengthen the draft of a speech I had written for delivery to the company Board of Directors. The subject was thermal oil recovery. I was told a head office guy was coming over to discuss the subject with me on a Friday. He appeared wearing the head office attire reserved for the big boys — white shoes and a matching white belt, partially visible beneath his bulging midsection. He seemed all the more ridiculous in contrast to the Rocky Mountain Drilling types I had just been working with on a recent trip to an oil field. It was going all right until it became clear that another person would be presenting my material and that the revised draft would be needed Monday morning. Unlike my first departure from Shell eight years earlier, this time a position was on offer from a small consulting firm in the petroleum industry. I said, "No can do." That moment was the end of my Shell career.

Keith Coats co-founded Intercomp Resource Development and Engineering, Inc. in 1968, after leaving professorships at the University of Michigan and the University of Texas at Austin. Much of the software written by Coats ultimately found its way to the major energy service companies of today, including Baker Hughes, Schlumberger and Halliburton Energy Services. He is the pioneering individual responsible for demonstrating the usefulness of the technology within the petroleum industry. He personally was the first to develop complex computer programs that allowed simulation of the recovery of heavy oil using steam injection and other thermal recovery methods. Intercomp was privately owned and headquartered in Houston, with satellite offices in Calgary and London. Coats worked solo, usually writing and testing code all night at the office, leaving bleary eyed and looking haggard when the rest of us were arriving for the day. His ability to quickly rejuvenate himself was uncanny. When he arrived in his growling Lamborghini late in the day to pull another all-nighter, he looked remarkably refreshed and much younger than his years. He had been a collegiate gymnast and it was rumored that his fountain of youth was a world-class home gymnasium. Coats reached the pinnacle of success, being named to the U.S. National Academy of Engineering in 1989, ten years after selling his company, and two years before my Berkeley thesis advisor would reach the same apex of engineering excellence. Until his passing in 2016, Coats lived on an island off Florida, enjoying the success of his applied genius, still writing code and performing as a technical man in his privately held company.

Reservoir simulation software is complex. A deep knowledge of mathematics, physics and chemical engineering is required to write the computer code, and awareness of programming subtleties developed over decades is necessary to achieve acceptably rapid processing speeds on the world's fastest computer clusters. Computer programming skills per se are secondary. Only a handful of men have been successful in writing such software, as evidenced by the annual licensing and maintenance fees of millions of dollars paid by a single big petroleum company for use of the code. There are a series of different oil recovery processes and a unique simulator is required for evaluation of each of them. One recovery process involves natural pressure depletion, another the injection of water, another carbon dioxide or enriched gas, another steam, another surfactant and so on. The Intercomp business model was to develop this chain of simulators and to lease or perpetually license the object code while charging an annual fee to maintain it. It was not possible for a customer to have access to the source code, which prevented him from altering it or profiting from its use.

At the same time, in-house consultants generated revenue by applying the simulators on projects for clients worldwide.

While at Shell Development Company, I met two men who as future business partners would become like brothers. Mike Todd and Curtis Chase had also worked in the group headed by Bill Miller. They were atypical, in that they were the most talented in the group and serious about the demanding work, yet at the same time knew how to enjoy life. Chase had been a chess champion and national merit scholarship winner from the state of Florida. Upon graduation from the Illinois Institute of Technology with a PhD in chemical engineering and another PhD in math, he served in Army Intelligence in Germany. He lived on a modest farm outside of Houston, had horses, pumped iron and hung-out with tobacco chewing good old boys, like some of those I had met at Rocky Mountain Drilling. When asked by his red-neck pals what he did for a living, Curtis Chase would answer in a way that left them thinking he pumped gas at a Shell service station. Anything other than a ladies man, when seen with a female companion she was a stunner, usually one of the department secretaries. He loved poker, a passion which saw him move to Reno, Nevada, during the last years of his life where he competed with the big talent. This is a personal profile that belies his standing as a top engineer, the best I ever knew. Mike Todd had also been a national merit scholarship winner from the state of Florida. He would later be introduced to Chase at Shell Development Company where they became very close friends. There was a brotherly love between the two of them, a healthy and inseparable bond that was constant until Chase's death in 2009. Todd attended the Massachusetts Institute of Technology, competing collegiately in swimming, specializing in the butterfly. Graduating with a degree in astronautical engineering he went on to earn a PhD in chemical engineering from the State University of New York at Buffalo. Todd is the eldest of three brothers. He had natural leadership qualities and would become our best contract negotiator. He would go on to receive the 2008 Society of Petroleum Engineers Pioneer Award for career-long distinguished contributions and dedication to improved oil recovery technology and processes.

While I was struggling as a division reservoir engineer, the two of them moved from their Big Oil research positions to the little *think tank* that was Intercomp. Enhanced oil recovery technology was exploding and Todd was one of few experts in the field of miscible flooding, a process that involves the injection of either carbon dioxide or enriched hydrocarbon gas to improve oil recovery. He had received a prestigious award from the Society of Petroleum Engineers for the best technical paper written by an author under age 33. He was a hot commodity and Intercomp recruited him to develop a chemical flood simulator. Todd in turn recruited Chase several months later to help with the project.

I left Shell Oil Company in 1977 and was excited to join them. Thermal oil recovery was my specialty, learned while working for a decade in the heavy oil fields of California. A thermal simulator was one of the most difficult to develop. Keith Coats had developed the only one available in the industry. It was my job to grow the business by applying thermal reservoir simulation for clients worldwide. My career dream had come true! I secured several projects domestically and one in Ankara, Turkey. Then the unexpected happened: Intercomp was sold to the publicly traded Kanab Coal Company in 1978. When that happened, it quickly changed from a think tank where the emphasis had been on individualism and creativity to one where the emphasis was on groups of people and quarterly earnings. No longer could one start the day by reading technical literature and discussing it with colleagues, there was an urgency to get work out the door. New additional bosses appeared, a marketing group was formed and soon billable time was not sufficient to pay the overhead. There was no oil coming out of the ground to cover it all and Intercomp was eventually sold to Scientific Software Inc., a consulting firm in Denver.

The three of us met every Friday after work for a beer outside the 7-Eleven™ convenience store near the Intercomp office. It was Chase who first raised the idea of breaking away, saying that we could compete with the Intercomp business model. We asked advice on how to proceed from prior colleagues who had left Shell Development Company to form their own highly successful earth science consultancy. Key inputs were to structure our little company as a C-corporation, retain professional legal and accounting services on a regular basis and share the profits equally. We carefully followed this advice. Houston was the energy capital of the world, replete with all types of consultants who could provide the necessary services. There was no way we were going out on our own without having our own software to compete in the new, rapidly emerging reservoir simulation space. It was too risky. Curtis Chase began developing a thermal simulator during nights and weekends while we all continued our day jobs at Intercomp for several more months.

CHAPTER THREE

LEAVING SECURITY

Todd, Dietrich & Chase, Inc. was formed on January 17, 1979 when our thermal simulator had come to life. Although this date happened to coincide with the day the Shah of Iran was forced into exile, there was nothing repressive about our employer and we were not revolting. We simply wanted to be bossless. Days earlier we announced our intention to leave Intercomp in a late afternoon meeting with Keith Coats and two of his vice presidents. There was a sense of surprise and annoyance, yet the mood was not unfriendly. I recall being told that chances of our success were not good and that we were making a mistake. We quickly began marketing our services domestically and abroad. We were on fire from the start. Our first three clients were heavy oil operators in California. The thermal reservoir simulator that Chase had written and the expertise to run it were the keys to securing these contracts. When Intercomp learned of our rapid and growing success, they cried foul, claiming our thermal simulator had been stolen from them! They demanded to see our source code and we quickly obliged, laying out our code next to theirs in a side by side comparison in our office, which was above the garage of Todd's residence. It was an awkward but not bitter demonstration. When it was clear there was no similarity of the software, we were absolved of guilt. We thought it best not to ask for an apology.

TDC next built a miscible flood simulator that became the industry standard for the design and evaluation of CO_2 injection projects. Its formulation was based on a wish list of features described by researchers from seven major oil companies in a meeting at our offices. It was a perfect coalition of three. Chase developed, installed and maintained the software, Todd took the lead on miscible flooding projects and I took the lead on thermal recovery projects. They were the theoreticians and I was the partner who understood the oil patch with a sense of how to market our skills. Americans led the world in the new reservoir simulation technology and totally dominated in the field of EOR, our specialty. The French had the Institute Francais du Petrole (IFP) with great engineers and a simulator or two that were not commercially available. Only Intercomp and Scientific-Software were serious competition. They were bloated with big staffs and high overhead. They would soon merge. We had nearly 60 clients after eight years, more than a third located outside of the United States in Australia, Canada, Europe and South America. They ranged in size from tiny Double Barrel Oil Company to Exxon. Unlike in the United States, it is rare for privately owned companies in other countries of the world to own mineral rights. It was much easier for us to start up and thrive with our business model than it would have been for a foreign competitor. Our domestic market was indeed broad and many of our clients were small, privately held companies.

M. H. Whittier Company was family owned and it became one of our earliest clients. Family members owned nearly all the stock in Belridge Oil Company, which held a giant shallow oil field in the San Joaquin Valley of California. One of its two major reservoirs contained heavy oil, where steam injection had been used to recover viscous oil for more than a decade. The company had a new chief engineer, a Stanford petroleum engineering graduate who had been working internationally for Occidental Petroleum. He sensed that oil recovery could be improved greatly by doing something different and he knew that the fresh reservoir simulation technology might be helpful. Mike Todd and I were asked to fly from Houston to Los Angeles to describe what we might do for them. We were to meet at their office in the oil field. All travel arrangements would be taken care of, there would be no reason for concern. Upon arrival in Los Angeles after flying first-class, we were met by limousine and driven to the exclusive Jonathan Club for lunch, where I still recall the beautiful, wood carved ceiling in the dining room and the smell of old money. Our host for that day and others to come was James Greene, the executive vice president of Belridge Oil. Just after earning a business degree from Oregon State University in 1941, Greene had volunteered for service in the U.S. Navy after Pearl Harbor, where he participated in major engagements in the South China Sea and South Pacific. Upon returning from the war, he got a job in the accounting office of M. H. Whittier Company. It quickly became apparent that Greene had a deep knowledge of lots of subjects, including petroleum engineering. There would be no blowing smoke by him during our marketing presentation, or at any other time. After lunch we flew via the corporate French Falcon jet to land beside the pumping units of the oil field, before being driven a short distance on dirt roads to the field office in two baby blue Mercedes Benz field cars. We were briefly introduced to Paul Whittier, the chairman of M. H. Whittier Company and philanthropist of repute, who was walking through the office on a cane, in a tattered sweater with his golden retriever leading the way. He was the first of three billionaire clients. The second would be a Russian oligarch in Moscow and the third a Dane in Copenhagen. The meeting went well with good humor being shared by all. It had been agreed before the trip that our time that day would be non-billable — it was a marketing trip. As we were boarding the French Falcon for the return flight to Los Angeles, we were jokingly offered carrots and cabbage as payment for our consulting time. M. H. Whittier Company of course had both the surface and mineral rights in the field and their agricultural business was mushrooming. A few days later our written proposal was accepted and we got the project, apparently in the absence of competitive bidding. After several months we demonstrated with thermal reservoir simulation that oil recovery would likely increase rapidly in response to injecting steam in a different way.

The chief engineer had the authority and funding to make the changes quickly, and he did. Less than a year later when the oil rate was nearly doubling every other month, the M. H. Whittier Corporation sold Belridge Oil to Shell Oil Company for 3.65 billion dollars, then the largest merger of two companies in the United States. Not surprisingly, James Greene capably handled the entire transaction himself. Years later, Charlie Munger, the long time business partner of Warren Buffet reportedly said, "The problem with closed bid auctions is that they are frequently won by people making a technical mistake, as in the case with Shell paying double for Belridge. You can't pay double the losing bid in an open outcry auction." It was Greene who had called for a closed bid auction! As wise as Munger is, this comment calling into question Shell's judgment may not be justifiable. There are two reservoirs in the Belridge field, the upper one contains the heavy oil that was being developed at the time in a series of unconsolidated sands. Beneath the sands is a thick, very tight reservoir containing both light and heavy oil in an unusual rock type called diatomite, formed by plankton that have settled to the bottom of the seafloor over geologic time. Mobil had just demonstrated a year before the sale that the billions of barrels of oil in the diatomite reservoir were producible, using hydraulic fracturing technology, now known to the general public as fracking. It would have been impossible to keep secret the results of their pilot fracturing test. It's likely that Shell placed significant value on the diatomite owing to this information and research that was underway at Shell Development Company to define its potential. Over the last two decades, Shell has drilled and hydraulically fractured more than 250 horizontal wells in the diatomite and is continuing to produce a lot of oil from them.

The great potential for improving oil recovery at Belridge was obvious from the moment we saw the data. Reflecting a price of 29 cents for each barrel of oil underneath the surface, the company stock was greatly undervalued. I had considered buying some of it but did not do so. My uncle had attended Stanford business school before leaving early to take over the security business from his father. He had been warned, and in turn warned me, about the dire consequences of insider trading during more than one of our late night chats. Munger must have passed on an opportunity to increase his stake for a different reason. He bought 300 shares of the thinly traded Belridge Oil stock in 1977 for 115 dollars per share. He later made public that one of his biggest mistakes was opting not to buy an additional 1,500 shares offered at the time. The stock price was 3,700 dollars per share two years later when some of the results of our project had been put into operation. At that time the oil rate was rapidly rising and the company was sold to Shell Oil.

The Belridge project put smiles on our faces and money in our coffers, allowing us to move into leased office space in Houston. It was followed by another heavy oil project, this one to last for several years. Like the Coalinga Polymer Demonstration Project, this venture involved field pilot testing of a novel oil recovery process, qualifying for partial funding from the U.S. Department of Energy. An entrepreneur had formed a corporation called Barber HOP (heavy oil process) Company, together with the two patent owners of the technology, men who had recently left geology professorships at the University of Texas. The technology involved drilling a vertical shaft to the base of a heavy oil accumulation, followed by rotary drilling horizontal wells from inside a bell-shaped chamber excavated at the bottom of the shaft. The horizontal wells were drilled at 45 degree increments from each other, ending with what looked in plan view like 8 spokes of a wagon wheel. This was followed by drilling 8 conventional vertical wells, one located in each of the eight wedges or sectors bounded by a pair of horizontals. The concept was to inject steam into the vertical wells and produce the heated oil of reduced viscosity from the horizontal wells. A horizontal well had been drilled a year earlier in Canada using modern technology, but never before in the United States, nor anywhere else in the world. This would be one of only two early demonstrations of horizontal well technology that more than a decade later would revolutionize the oil industry.

Barber HOP had selected a property available from Shell Oil Company in the Kern River field of California as the demonstration site. The major contractor on the project brought in drilling equipment from Nevada that had been used decades earlier to drill the big-diameter boreholes for holding and testing nuclear bombs. Following a speech and celebration with a Department of Energy dignitary breaking a bottle of champagne against the drilling assembly, the 7-foot diameter shaft was drilled to its planned depth of 500 feet and miners were lowered to excavate the 25-ft diameter bell-shaped chamber. Before the shaft was cased and lined with concrete, I accepted an offer to be lowered by cable into the newly excavated chamber, there to view and describe the geology where the steam would be injected. There was a problem! The horizontal production wells were going to be placed directly below a tight interval of rock which would impede the gravity drainage of heated oil from the overlying heavy oil sands. The tight zone had an easily recognizable signature on the electrical logs, which had been obtained not only in four new core holes drilled for the pilot, but also in numerous old wells drilled decades earlier. The well control showed that the non-reservoir sediments are present as discontinuous lenses, not as layers continuous over the 25-acre demonstration site. The industry was aware that these same discontinuous lenses are present over much of the Kern River field, and that steam injected below them quickly segregates upward to accumulate at the top of the reservoir. Perhaps it was this awareness that led to a lack of concern about the possible impedance effects of the lenses on the drainage of hot oil. After all, it's the same geological system — if steam moves easily upward, hot oil should drain easily downward. More likely, it was simply that the already published effect of overlapping shale on effective vertical permeability, and its implication relating to achievable drainage rates, had been missed by the HOP design team.

TDC had been brought into the project after the design had been completed. Our job was to use the new technology of thermal reservoir simulation to predict the likely oil recovery volumes — that is, the proved reserves — over time in response to different steam injection schedules. The elevation of the wells to be drilled could not be changed as the shaft and chamber were already in place. As with the polymer project designed by Shell Development Company, there were very capable civil and chemical engineers on the project and the contract geologist was highly qualified, but none of them had a practical background in both engineering and geology that allowed them to see the reservoir for what it was, and what it needed to be. In order to achieve commercial production rates, few low permeability strata could be present which would impede the gravity drainage process. The pilot project produced at sluggish rates predicted by the simulator during the next year or two, before being shut-in due to uneconomic oil rates. Sadly, the entrepreneur declared bankruptcy. He was able to ultimately settle all claims at 90 cents on the dollar, becoming my only client in 40 years who did not pay the full amount of an invoice. The Barber HOP technology was a technical success but an economic failure. It was placed in the wrong geological setting. A decade and a half later, topdrive drilling rig technology was introduced, allowing horizontal wells to be drilled from the surface using what are called double-tilted U-joint, steerable motors. There was no longer a need to drill a shaft and substitute mining personnel for oilfield workers to excavate a chamber.

Trinidad Tesoro Petroleum Company was our first foreign client. Located in Santa Flora, Trinidad, they produced heavy oil using steam injection technology. In response to a marketing cold call, I was invited to visit them for the purpose of describing how thermal reservoir simulation might be used to improve their operations. On our own company expenses, this time it was an economy class flight to Miami and then on to Port of Spain, Trinidad. I recall there was a standup bar on the aircraft leaving Miami, where passengers unknown to each other would mingle, swilling free sparkling wine and revealing more about themselves than is discreet, in a way that flying can promote. It was a pleasant flight. Upon arrival, I checked into the upside-down Hilton hotel that is built on the side of a mountain, where all rooms are accessed by taking an elevator down to them from the registration area. The view from the balcony of my room was of an expansive area hundreds of feet below holding a series of sports fields, including those for horse racing, polo, cricket and football. That first night, traveling alone and unmet by my client, I headed via taxi to a small restaurant outside of the city, selected at the recommendation of the taxi driver. Few people were in the place. I sat on a stool at the bar where the food was served, bantering for hours with the female staff dressed in attractive bright colors, while trying not to stare at their inches-long finger nails. When it was time to return to the upside-down place, I asked if a taxi might be called for me. The answer was, "No." It was too dangerous and someone from the restaurant would drive me to the hotel. I must have come across as the trusting and naive Forrest Gump type that I am, and they liked me. I left a good tip. The hotel staff soon had a very amusing time telling me I had chosen a brothel for a restaurant.

Early the next morning I hired a driver endorsed by the hotel to chauffer me to my meeting in Santa Flora, located on the south end of the island 50 miles away. My client was the general manager of the company. His name was Mr. Ablack, a native of Trinidad, quiet and smart looking with thick eyeglasses. He asked during our introduction whether my brother was in the petroleum business. They liked his paper published years earlier on oil well casing stresses and used his findings in their work. It was off to a good start! Before the day was over, I had given a presentation describing thermal reservoir simulation to his staff and obtained enough information to prepare a business proposal describing how we might help them improve oil recovery from the Guapo field with less steam usage. I recall giving the presentation with heavy rainfall pounding on a tin roof held up on posts, not walls. A sea of shiny, focused faces signaled interest in my material and I had to speak loudly to be heard. The proposal was written upon my return to Houston and forwarded via DHL courier. It was quickly accepted and two months later I returned to the island with the results, this time with my two daughters in tow, ages 11 and 13. I felt comfortable accepting an invitation to leave them with my driver's family in Port of Spain while the driver and I were in Santa Flora for the day. Upon our return in the evening to his home, a plate of fruit was on offer while all of us shared the news of the day. It was covered black with flies and I was unsure of how to proceed without offending our hosts. My girls looked at me for a tip-off on what to do. I am unable to recall how we got past that moment. Perhaps it was by focusing on the excitement of their day, which involved witnessing the wringing of chickens' necks in preparation of our hosts' evening meal. There was no lasting trauma, for that night at the hotel restaurant my daughters chose chicken from the menu. They were given a gift by one of the kitchen staff we had met at breakfast. It was a record album from an artist on the nearby island of Jamaica who was exploding in popularity. It was an autographed album by Bob Marley, the reggae king. On the way to our room after dinner, a woman dressed to the nines was standing alone on a small bridge along our path, her perfume and lipstick heavy and smile awkward. When my younger daughter asked why she was standing there, I am again unable to recall how we got past a second tricky moment.

Trinidad Tesoro listened to my suggestions on how to improve their steam injection profiles that were based on thermal reservoir simulation. The payoff would likely be more oil production per volume of steam injected.

Their real interest though was in getting help with computer technology. Several months later I introduced my friend Odis Wooten to Trinidad Tesoro on a return marketing trip. Odis had recently started the original Computer Technology Associates Inc. in Houston and was the right man for the job. We traveled together at holiday time, arriving a few weeks before Christmas when the upside-down Hilton was booked with one party after another. The night of our arrival, we, absent invitation, joined a huge group in a ballroom where the lights were low and the music loud, thinking we would not be noticed. When Odis split open his only pair of pants while on the dance floor, it all turned bad. Finding a tailor before our meeting the next day was the least of our problems. Perhaps the group of local blokes thought we were trying to get naked with their women, when they approached insisting we should leave at once. I was learning that Trinidad could be a tough place, especially for a couple of suits in the wrong hood.

Odis was introduced the next day, making a fine impression with his pants in good repair. Our host that day heading the IT Department was a rough and ready type, who as a field man did not seem right for the job. He insisted during our meeting that we get together that evening at his establishment near Santa Flora, ostensibly to continue talking business. We understood there would be a dinner on offer. The place was like out of a western movie, with swinging louvered doors at the entrance and sawdust covering wooden plank floors. A bottle of whiskey was placed on a rough wooden table upon our arrival, before the potential client began calling ladies from upstairs to begin their parade by us, one by one. It was soon clear that the overpriced bottle of whiskey was going on our tab. Moreover, we were each to choose a minimum of two ladies for the evening, as the price for proceeding further with negotiation of a contract. I do recall how this third tricky moment on the island of Trinidad was passed. We declined and headed unfulfilled back to the hotel for dinner, knowing that our business in Trinidad was done. It had been a great trip overall for Odis and myself. We had a lot of fun, especially for a couple of STEM guys.

Our second foreign contract was with a German company. It also ended in an inelegant manner, but this time it had nothing to do with offered bribery. Wintershall AG is headquartered in Kassel, Germany, the home of the Grimms Brothers of fairytale fame. There is little oil in Germany, requiring that country to focus on developing a synthetic fuels industry. A lot of heavy oil had been discovered in the Emsland area near the Dutch border prior to World War II. However, it was so viscous that it would only dribble into the wellbores, leading the Third Reich to open an eastern front where access to oil from the Caucasus became the primary objective. Thermal oil recovery was recognized as a viable technology for recovering heavy oil in 1962, when Shell Oil Company injected steam into a well in Venezuela to clean the casing perforations. Upon returning the well to production after a few days of shut-in, it began flowing at surprisingly high oil rates. This type of cyclic process is still widely used today and it often precedes application of a process called steam flooding, where steam is injected continuously. The Germans began steam flooding the Emlichheim heavy oil field in 1981 after using natural depletion and hot water flooding to recover minor amounts of oil after the war. There was still a lot of oil left. In response to my telephone marketing call from Houston, I was invited to visit them to describe how thermal reservoir simulation could improve their operations. I recall flying on the German carrier Lufthansa and being invited to upgrade from coach to business class at no charge, simply because my family name is Dietrich. That was a good start. Upon arrival in Frankfurt, I hired a taxi for a ride of an hour, or more, to Kassel. Dozing in the back seat, I caught a glimpse of a Porsche rocketing by and was astonished, not by the more than 130 mph speed itself, but by the combination of speed and road conditions — snow and ice covered the sides of the autobahn. The taxi ride was expensive and not repeated, as train service was good. I met the chief reservoir engineer on that trip, a person who would bring more business my way than any other over the next two decades. His name is Ivan de Grisogono, a Serb originally from Belgrade, Yugoslavia. He had a twinkle in his eye, a great sense of humor and gravitas. Although Yugoslavia was starting to break apart at the time, we never spoke of it. And I don't know why. That business trip resulted in several projects and repeat travel to Kassel, where partner meetings starting early in the morning were attended by German engineers from Mobil AG, BEB Erdöl and Erdgas GmbH, and Preussag AG, co-owners of the heavy oil fields, with Wintershall acting as the remaining co-owner and operator. It was not unusual to view white knuckles and red faces upon first sitting down at the conference table, developed by those driving at high speeds into Kassel from offices in neighboring cities. Ivan also visited our office in Houston for a weeklong working session involving thermal reservoir simulation. On the second to last day of his visit, I suggested he move hotels, from a Hilton on the west side of the city to the Adam's Mark, just across the street. It was the weekend coming up before his return flight and I knew the Mark was a happening place, surely to be more fun for an unmarried man. The night of his move a fire broke out in the Hilton, killing two hotel guests while Ivan was safely ensconced and sleeping soundly across the street. There is no answer to the question of whether the move was based on premonition or just pure luck. In any event, Ivan displayed a loyalty to me in business for years to come, not only while at Wintershall, but also while employed elsewhere throughout his career. The last time I would see him for more than a decade was at a conference in Paris, where, unknown to me, he was also attending and giving a paper on one of our projects. I invited him and several other Wintershall men to join me at the Folies Bergere where we all enjoyed a last night in Paris.

Months later I heard that Ivan had moved on to another company in Germany. He was replaced by Gunther Proyer, an Austrian married to an Iranian woman, who introduced herself as Persian, working as a petroleum engineer and reporting to him, a wholly unacceptable business arrangement in the United States. When we were asked to have her work with us on a project in Houston for two months, it sounded like a tall order. As the client's wife, there was a lot that could go wrong, and it did. Upon her arrival, I had rented a car for her only to learn that she was not capable of driving, only steering the vehicle on a straight, lightly traveled road to and from her hotel located minutes away. The culture shock that was Houston was not easy for her, never mind the lack of any social life. Keith Coats had put in place a two-tier system for man-time consulting fees at Intercomp, where it was 90 dollars per hour absent the client and 120 dollars per hour given the client on site looking over your shoulder. We should have employed such a system. A problem arose toward the end of the project, when the thermal reservoir simulator began to run too slowly. It was having difficulty converging the equations describing fluid flow to an acceptable solution on each time step. This was not normal, but not unprecedented. It was no longer possible to get a prediction of reservoir performance overnight, by letting the simulator run on one of the world's most powerful computers as we slept. Instead it was taking several nights for the same interval of prediction. On this project we needed a really powerful computer. Boeing Aircraft Company in Seattle agreed to rent us excess capacity on one of their Cray supercomputers, a machine that sold for 8 to 10 million dollars at the time. The Germans had warned when preparing the purchase order for the project that the dollar number for computing, once fixed, could not be increased. We were paying Boeing 1,000 dollars per CPU-hour for computing time and we ran out of the computing budget, just prior to the scheduled return date of our guest client. She was not pleased when taken to the airport. A week later I flew to Kassel, there to present the final results, which had been obtained by hand-extrapolating trends established with the struggling simulator. The Germans were polite about it all, but did not return for business until more than two decades later. Perhaps it would have been sooner if Gunther had not taken his life by running a car engine with the garage door closed. He had unwittingly given a Nigerian scam artist access to his bank account, which was emptied of his company pension funds, reportedly leaving him in heavy depression. For a period of time, many of us in the industry received official looking letters from Nigerians asking for a temporary safe haven for their funds, with a promise for compensation.

The word simulate is defined as, "To assume the appearance of without the reality." On those few occasions when one outside the industry is interested in the topic of reservoir simulation, he commonly asks, "How good are the predictions of reservoir performance made with a simulator, anyway?" The question is usually unanswerable. This is because so many things are done differently in the years following a project than were assumed at the time of the prediction. I received a call from Shell Oil Company in 1986, asking if I might be available to once again look at the Alaskan reservoir that marked the first major simulation project for me and them. When carefully reviewing my report prepared 14 years earlier as a Shell employee, they had been astounded to observe a really good fit between actual and simulated oil rate over the history. I was astounded too! The project that marked a re-simulation of that Alaskan asset to study the merits of drilling additional wells was completed in 1987. The results were uncomfortable for Shell. They showed that Amoco, who operated two platforms at the ends of the long, narrow field for different owners, had installed more efficient artificial lift equipment on one of their platforms, allowing them to drain oil from the central portion of the field operated by Shell for more than two decades. Differences in operating techniques were certainly legal. There was no recourse for Shell. This would be my last project while employed at Todd, Dietrich & Chase, Inc.

CHAPTER FOUR

ON MY OWN

I sold my stock in Todd, Dietrich & Chase, Inc. and opened The Dietrich Corporation as a Sub-chapter S corporation in early 1987. Saudi Arabia began flooding the market with oil in late 1985. The world price of oil had peaked in 1980, a year after we started our consultancy, at more than $35 per barrel ($100 per barrel today). It fell in 1986 from 27 to below $10 per barrel (58 to $22 per barrel today). Our specialty, enhanced oil recovery, was decimated. We had no corporate debt and could most likely ride out the bad times. In my case, I needed to tap my profit sharing and pension plan to service on-going college tuition fees and expenses for three children. Cashing out was the least difficult option. Todd, Dietrich & Chase had been a tremendously successful company. I thought I could do as well on my own, and I did, but only because Todd and Chase agreed to make the simulators available to me on a rental basis, as needed. Becoming just another consultant without having a leg up on the competition would not have been a good move, especially during the severe industry downturn. The termination agreement was amicable, simple and straightforward, with very little money going for legal fees.

My first client was Crutcher-Tufts Corporation headquartered in New Orleans, Louisiana. Two geologists working for Standard Oil of California had become interested in developing a property on the edge of a major field that was too small for their employer. They left to start their own company, purchased the property, developed it and traded up for other oil leases over time, following a business model that is almost uniquely American. Albert Crutcher and David Tufts made it big, not quite to the billionaire status of the Whittier family, but they had owned a yacht recently sold to King Juan Carlos of Spain and owned two homes at Pebble Beach in California, where they frequently traveled to play golf. There was a big painting of the yacht on their office wall in New Orleans and they liked being asked about it.

They held a 320-acre lease in the Belridge field that contained light oil in the diatomite formation. Diatomite is a strange rock. When it is put under stress by withdrawing fluids from it, it compacts greatly, shrinking the thickness of the reservoir and causing surface subsidence. During one of my field visits, it was staggering to see an 18-wheeler that had mostly disappeared into a surface crevice. That was rare. Common were wells that had been destroyed by the shear stresses set up in the overburden above the compacting reservoir as oil was produced from them. The solution was to inject water to maintain reservoir pressure, thereby preventing the increase of stress and the incidence of well failures. I was hired to design a waterflood for the Crutcher-Tufts lease, using reservoir simulation. The project went well and the breaking of wellbores gradually stopped upon water flooding. Little did I know that diatomite would become a big part of my business life for the next half decade.

It was the prior agent of Double Barrel Oil Company who called, saying he was managing the lease for Crutcher-Tufts and needed help. My business dealings were with the son of the late co-founder of the company and an attorney. He was young and without experience in his position of authority, losing composure occasionally with the wrong person. One incident involving a heated verbal exchange with an agent of the California Division of Oil and Gas may have been the reason for an increased tax liability on the lease. It was a small family owned company. In the standard manner for both big and small companies, loans taken from the banks using future oil production as collateral generated pressure to inflate estimates of oil reserves. I was handling the preparation of the annual reserve report for a number of years, a responsibility that calls for an arms-length relationship with the client. It got to the point where a cut in booked reserves was necessary and that was difficult, especially since it was such a small company. I was not asked to prepare the reserve report after 1992. It was recently learned the company apparently filed for bankruptcy in the year 2008.

Other operators were beginning to develop the diatomite in the San Joaquin Valley and finding new wells breaking like matchsticks. Several leases had been producing for more than 5 years from wells drilled on 5/12 to 1¼-acre well spacing. More than 100 wells had been lost in the South Belridge field alone. That adage of the free market capitalist system, "Find a need and fill it," sparked an idea that gelled when meeting with a former Intercomp colleague at the Society of Petroleum Engineers (SPE) California Regional Meeting in 1988. Breaking wellbores were hugely expensive and a common problem, requiring a common solution for many companies. We formed a joint venture company and marketed an unsolicited consortium research project. Arco, Mobil, Unocal and Santa Fe Energy Resources signed a contract with us that called for more than a year of laboratory research work and reservoir simulation on diatomite. The project was called the California Diatomite Study Project (CDSP). We designed the laboratory programs and rented software from Schlumberger, who had purchased a simulator suitable for evaluating natural depletion and water injection processes, as a first step in their development of an Intercomp type of business model. That simulator was simple when compared to those needed for evaluation of EOR processes, but it was highly stable and reliable. It was largely developed by the late Ian Cheshire, who left the British Atomic Energy Authority in 1981 to begin its development.

Each of the client companies co-funded the consortium research project in equal amounts. The project was novel and the participants enjoyed meeting monthly to hear progress reports at the Hilton hotel adjacent to the Los Angeles International Airport, a convenient meeting location for project participants from California, Colorado, Pennsylvania, Texas and Alberta, Canada. On my own and several months later, I prepared and submitted another unsolicited proposal to a group of companies, including three of the former clients that owned heavy oil diatomite properties where steam injection was needed for oil recovery. What was different in this proposed project was the addition of thermal effects to the problem. It was known to a few of us that when steam is injected into diatomite, it greatly accelerates its rate of compaction. That key phenomenon was explained in a confidential report written by a researcher at Shell Development Company, a document that had begun appearing on desks of its competitors about the time I prepared my proposal. It was so widely available, with the cover sheet and word "Confidential" long missing, that I referenced it in my tender and foolishly included Shell on my mailing list. A friend at Shell Development Company called while I was vacationing in Hawaii, saying that Shell was furious with this breach of confidentiality and was preparing to sue me. They thought I had stolen the report that was written two years after my exit from Shell. I took this seriously and telephoned the document's author, who was well known to me, explaining that the entire industry had a copy of his work and that a client had given me my copy. The incident was dropped before it became one.

There is no way to control the long term compaction and surface subsidence effects of steam injection in diatomite. The objective of the proposed work was to predict how much deformation was likely to occur, and when, given different field development plans. The California Diatomite Thermal Study Project (CDTSP) was more complex in scope, requiring the compaction thermal simulator that Curtis Chase had previously developed for application in Venezuela. The concern there had been to prevent the Orinoco

River from overflowing into the adjacent heavy oil fields, where thermally-induced compaction and surface subsidence were occurring due to thermal oil recovery. Arco, Mobil, Texaco and Unocal signed up and co-funded the CDTSP project that ran for two years. Monthly progress meetings were held at the Rio Bravo Country Club in Bakersfield, a pleasant resort that looked out onto the Kern River oil field. The compaction thermal simulator was rented from Todd and Chase and the computer budget included $50,000 of Cray supercomputer time from Texas A&M University. Laboratory work was undertaken at two commercial labs and three universities, including my undergraduate alma mater, U.C. Santa Barbara, where I retained the very same professor of geology who had not allowed me to take his petrology course, because he did not have enough expensive petrographic microscopes. The class size had to be limited and I was the student on probation.

While sitting in my office in Durango, Colorado, feeling the pinch of the Saudi oil flood and wondering how long it was going to last, I decided to propose another private consortium research project. This time the prospective clients would be German oil companies that operate steam injection projects in the heavy oil reservoirs of the Emsland area, including my prior client Wintershall and its co-owners of the Emlichheim field. There are several heavy oil reservoirs in that region, each underlain by a huge, common aquifer and each operated by a different company. While working on the Emlichheim project, I realized that all of the operators were facing a common problem that was growing and self-imposed. They were injecting more steam and hot water than the oil and water they were producing, thereby gradually increasing the reservoir pressure over time. In steam flooding, oil recovery and thermal efficiency are both greatly increased at low, rather than high, reservoir pressure. The objective is to operate in a manner that maintains a low reservoir pressure. The common solution to this problem was to stop re-injecting the produced water back into the reservoir. Instead, after separating the produced water from the oil, it could be cleaned and disposed of on the surface, either into streams and lakes or artificial storage ponds, or used for agricultural purposes. At the same time, a number of wells would need to be drilled into the aquifer and pumped to de-pressure it. I needed a partnering company that was qualified to provide the mechanical and civil engineering elements of the project. After developing a draft proposal, I contacted Mannesmann AG of Dusseldorf and, surprisingly, they agreed to partner on the consortium research proposal. Our comprehensive tender was ready after 3 months of preparation. It was presented in Hanover to about 20 engineers representing 5 different companies. It was well received with pounding of fists on the conference table in the German tradition showing high approval. However, no company signed up for the project, citing uncertainty about oil prices as the reason. The result was like the HOP demonstration project, it was a promising technical concept but an economic failure. It was very disappointing. I had never spent so much time and money on developing and marketing a business proposal.

BP would be my next client. It was just in time when the phone rang, as the money coffers were nearly empty. Many colleagues were getting out of the oil industry altogether, more than a few buying almond orchards in the Great Valley of California and becoming farmers. There had been up and down cycles earlier, but not like this. The caller was a former colleague at Intercomp. He asked, "Are you available to work with BP in Houston to design an EOR project for one of their Alaskan reservoirs?" The next week, the Houstonian Hotel & Club, situated on 18 private, heavily treed acres just blocks from BP's offices became my new home. It was quiet and its sports club was world class, known to me as a club member while living previously in Houston. I negotiated an affordable rate for a long-term stay in a quiet, 2nd floor hotel corner room, with light coming in from windows on two walls and beautiful views of post oak and pine trees, my favorite. I rented a big desk and chair from a furniture company, and used them for working nights and weekends on the diatomite research project after my day job in BP's offices. I was finding it necessary to work two projects at one time on my own, or else lose half of the business in-hand.

President George Herbert Walker Bush and his wife made the Houstonian their Texas residence. They had to be there a number of days each year to maintain legal Texas residency. A few weeks before each presidential visit, the U.S. Secret Service would swarm over the hotel, knocking holes in the walls for communications cables and interviewing residents in the few neighboring high rise buildings, all with a sense of urgency and highest purpose. It was disruptive. It was prestigious to host the president, but the hotel actually lost money during these visits. The president played tennis and liked a bowl of vanilla ice cream, late every night. When my room was needed for the presidential entourage while I was in California on diatomite business, I was told that simply placing my personal items under cover in the corner of the room would be fine. I received a call from the Houstonian while in California, asking if my things could be temporarily moved into storage. As the Gulf War had started, I gladly obliged, to do my small part. My choice corner room was occupied by Nicholas Brady, the Secretary of the Treasury, who must have appreciated having more space and the use of a big desk. Upon my return, I was given a dark blue fountain pen with a presidential seal on it. It leaked ink while in my dress shirt pocket and I threw it away.

My position was in the Reservoir Technology Department at BP, a group headed by Will Culham, a bespectacled, intelligent looking man with an Einstein hair style who was American and all business. He had a floor to ceiling bookcase in his office that covered one complete wall, containing leather bound editions of the classic technical literature of our industry, most of which he had carefully read. He was a very serious man and the place was run like a tight ship in those areas where he had control. The group was staffed by a myriad of PhDs from all over the world, giving it a United Nations feel.

There were Russians, Nigerians, Chinese, British and North Americans. The project was a huge success and I felt right at home, never mind that a few names were placed on my final report who had little or nothing to do with it, in the top billing spots. It was simply corporate politics. Keith Coats's daughter worked at BP, an attractive, bright person and very competent chemical engineer, who during my contract period left Big Oil to get married and move to Cleveland, Ohio. Culham left months after the completion of my last of three projects to open a consultancy in Dallas. When he invited me to join him, I declined, only because there could be no better small, high technology group than Todd, Dietrich & Chase, Inc., and that had been the best of memories. I did not bump into my former partners in the business world, probably because Chase rarely traveled and Todd and I had different technical specialties.

More than a decade later I would take a contract with BP at their North Sea Headquarters in Scotland, to work in a much different, less positive business culture. There are bitter and sweet memories of BP in Houston. Unfortunately, the bitter ones came last and they are unforgettable. During the last weeks of my contract in September, 1991, I answered a phone call while at my computer workstation. A voice said, "This is Constantine Nicandros." Of course I knew he was the president and CEO of Conoco; I didn't know how he found me. It felt strange, as if an omnipotent person could find me anywhere, anytime. Nicandros was calling from across town to say my brother's corporate aircraft was missing on the Tokyo to Jakarta leg of an around-the-world flight that would have put him in Dubai a few days later. The DuPont Gulfstream II jet had crashed into the side of a mountain in the Malaysian state of Sabah on the Island of Borneo, while attempting to land for scheduled refueling in Kota Kinabalu. All 12 people on board were killed, including my brother and sister-in-law, 3 crew members and 7 other Conoco executives and their wives. It was my role to call each of my family members, including my parents and brother's three children. There has never been a report issued about the investigation of this private plane crash, notwithstanding the unprecedented number of United States Federal agencies involved and the number of Federal employees sent to the site: six Consular Officers from the Department of State (DOS) and/or Central Intelligence Agency (CIA), one investigator from the National Transportation Safety Board (NTSB), two investigators from the Federal Aviation Administration (FAA), one investigator from the Federal Bureau of Investigation (FBI) and twelve investigators from the Office of Armed Forces Medical Examiner (OAFME). Why? Family members of the victims were told the crash was the result of a failure in air traffic control. They accepted financial settlements from the insurance carrier (AIG) with this understanding, unaware of the involvement of so many federal agencies and a massive cover-up that had just taken place.

The truth was not known until nearly 10 years later when Roger Parsons, whose wife died in the crash, described what happened in an article entitled, "The Iran-Conoco Affair." The piece reads like fiction, but all of it really happened. The final paragraph reads, "In the end, the DOS/CIA men that Bush sent to Malaysia recovered Dietrich's documents keeping Bush's involvement in the Iran-Conoco deal quiet. And, Nicandros, Rudge and Petersen successfully concealed and destroyed evidence that they knew would reveal the cause of the plane crash that killed twelve people they called 'friends.'"

Parsons also worked at Conoco, and although he is unknown to me, with a PhD in theoretical physics he must be highly intelligent and for sure he is dogged. When he began asking executive management at Conoco and DuPont (its parent company at the time) to investigate matters shortly after the catastrophe, he was fired. Parsons maintains a website and continues to petition authorities with the US FAA and NTSB, the Malaysian Attorney General, and the DuPont and ConocoPhillips Board of Directors, "To conduct a thorough investigation and issue a report on the circumstances of and causes for the DuPont-Conoco aircraft crash."

Following this tragedy, I organized my personal affairs and purchased additional life insurance. My days were filled with completing The California Diatomite Thermal Study Project, which was taking a lot of time. Each of the sponsoring companies had paid their share of the project in a series of 15 monthly payments. The laboratory experiments had taken longer than planned and the results were finally becoming available. It was a situation where no money was coming in, yet there was no problem, as the computing budget had been paid in advance and I had no payroll to meet. There was just me. I would arrive early at my office in Houston with The Dietrich Corporation name on the door, access the Cray supercomputer at Texas A&M using FTP (file transfer protocol) over phone lines for processing the simulations, eat a healthy lunch at The Houstonian and leave for a run around Memorial Park when the time was right. It seemed almost possible to become less serious and enjoy life more, vows I had made following the plane crash. The California Diatomite Thermal Study Project was to become the most complex and interesting technical project of my career. I had imagined it, marketed it, directed it and had performed all of the reservoir engineering and reservoir simulation work myself. It was also one of the least profitable projects of my career!

The problems caused by compacting diatomite reservoirs were so significant for the industry that a number of the Big Oil research labs were getting involved. I felt privileged to be invited as a speaker to a colloquium on reservoir compaction and surface subsidence hosted by Chevron Oil Field Research Company in La Habra, California during January, 1992. It's a date I remember because, on that trip to present a technical paper, I met a woman who would be sharing life and more than two decades of incredible expat adventures with me.

CHAPTER FIVE

MEETING THE ONE

My technical paper and 35-mm slides for a Kodak carousel projector were ready a week before my scheduled presentation at the Chevron Oil Field Research colloquium. There would be some powerful presentations at that venue, but I was confident that my material would be well received. The laboratory results were showing that diatomite compacts rapidly when the temperature of the reservoir is increased by steam injection. These were new data. The thermal reservoir simulator developed by Chase was uniquely formulated to model these creep effects, giving the lease operator an estimate of how changes in stress and the level of surface subsidence are related to time.

It was January and even Houston gets cold in the winter. I was ready for the colloquium. Why not first take time to get warm and relaxed on a brief vacation? I booked my flight to stop in Puerto Vallarta, Mexico, on my way to the southern California colloquium. Traveling with briefcase in hand, I checked into the resort, looking undoubtedly like the nerd I am. At least I was tie-less. I recall being relaxed, going for brisk early morning swims in a pool surrounded by second floor rooms with balconies, where guests would occasionally peer around the bougainvillea to watch the next Michael Phelps in action. It was probably noise from the splashing, shallow racing dives that brought out the few observers. Signs saying no diving were missing in Mexico. Several days were passed by playing volley ball in the pools with other guests and witnessing water polo matches that seemed almost world class in quality. It was always a group of collegiate looking American men versus young athletic Mexicans, more than just a series of pick up games, but not structured and not refereed. There were modified rules, no whistles and only a handful of resort guests were spectators. It was brutal competition, beyond the edge of good sportsmanship and the sense was the matches took place regularly. I took room service for dinner on two of my three nights, not accepting invitations to join others for too much tequila and mariachi music. I was comfortable and not self conscious that I was on my own, perhaps because I was approaching the age of 50. An advertising commercial for a new Canon camera had Andre Agassi declaring at the time, "Image Is Everything," a message that now missed me completely.

Prior to leaving for the airport I went for a jog and changed into slacks, one of those polo shirts with a little alligator on it and loafers. I was tan, lean and fit, and life was great. While seated in the waiting area for the flight, I was reading "Ford: The Man and The Machine," a biography that had come off the best sellers' list four years earlier. A flash of turquoise caught my eye in the color of a jacket worn by a woman coming down some wide stairs into the waiting room. She was gorgeous, tall, with long slender legs that were revealed in well tailored black slacks when she leaned over at a drinking fountain. She was traveling with an older woman and apparently without a man. The flight was late, and there was more than a little time to look her way upon glancing up from reading about Henry. Other men, and much of the entire waiting room, were looking at us when she stopped to ask me the time of day, upon her return from another drinking fountain pose. Her eyes got to me. She later said she really liked my briefcase and shoes. Ah, the difference between men and women. I asked her, "Would you like to have a beverage?" While sipping our Gatorade sports drinks in the absence of her mother, who was left in the waiting area, I asked about her views of Anita Hill, who had just gone public alleging that Clarence Thomas, a nominee for the supreme court put forth by George Herbert Walker Bush, had grabbed her butt on more than one occasion while she had worked for him at the U.S. Department of Education and the Equal Employment Opportunity Commission. Well, in defense of such a question, I didn't have much time to know if I wanted to get to know this woman whose eyes had captivated me. The plane would soon be at the gate. She answered that Anita, as a Harvard PhD, who had signed up for repeated postings under Thomas, was strong enough to have handled it all without crying sexual harassment. That sounded good, even through the fog of a Gatorade high.

There was no chance to sit next to her on the full flight. Instead I had to listen to some lothario talk about how he had scored repeatedly while in Puerto Vallarta. I think he was puffing himself up, as the older man had been singled out rather than himself to meet the gorgeous potential date at the gate.

I telephoned her from Houston after returning from a successful colloquium, inviting her to join me for dinner and a stage play two weeks later in Los Angeles, near her residence in Beverly Hills. When I told my daughters of this, they insisted I call her back at once, explaining that the evening was to be a celebration of my 50th birthday. The special evening was being arranged by my sister who lived in Pasadena, California. Present that evening would be my mother, father, sister, brother-in-law, and two of my three daughters, all being chauffer driven in a limousine, a first for me. No matter that upon arrival her Beverly Hills address was a rented unit in a 4-unit complex. Never mind that the imagined butler answering the door with white gloves in a home without the odor of a cat box was a fiction, her eyes kept shining through. This was a strong, intelligent woman, who while returning in the filled limo asked, "How did I do on a scale of 1 to 10?" My father who was hard of hearing answered, "2," thinking she had simply asked, "Choose a number between 1 and 10." She handled that effortlessly, and all else that evening, with humor. Her social skills were off the chart. I knew she liked my family, and I sensed she liked the man behind the briefcase.

We were married four months later in Salzburg, Austria, a favorite romantic, small city of population 150,000, discovered after one of my business trips to Wintershall, in Kassel, Germany. When I telephoned to make a June reservation for the wedding ceremony at a place called Mirabell Palace, there were no dates available. When it was learned the reservation would be under the name Dietrich, the tone quickly changed from polite to almost obsequious and our request was met. The change was puzzling. When we arrived, all became clear. Prince-Archbishop Wolfgang Dietrich had Mirabell Palace built for Salome Alt, his mistress, in the year 1606. Mirabell today houses the offices of Salzburg's mayor and municipal council. The wedding ceremony took place in The Marble Hall, formerly Wolfgang Dietrich's ballroom and concert hall for Leopold Mozart.

Upon our return, we sold homes in Houston and Durango, Colorado and rented an old carriage house in Santa Barbara, California, whose previous occupant had been a Schlumberger heiress. It was a cool place, with a front door that slid open and closed in a sideways motion on a top guide rail, not a candidate for purchase due to termite damage. The main estate house had burned down decades earlier and had not been replaced. It had been difficult to find a suitable rental while we looked for the right home to buy. Owners had tapped into home equity when home prices were higher and now many were upside down. It seemed lots of people had a HELOC (home equity line of credit) in Santa Barbara. Unable to sell, their only option was to rent their home or give it back to the bank. We learned quickly to ask if an owner was planning to live on the rental property, either above the garage or in an outbuilding of some type. Absent an absent owner, we passed on a rental opportunity. Our landlord owned negative equity on her carriage house. She had chosen to stay with a friend while renting her home and living on a book advance from a publishing house. Upon reading a draft of her manuscript, it seemed her problems were not going to be over soon.

The carriage house is a two story residence. The main level houses the living area and kitchen, from which there is a partial view of the pacific ocean. Two bedrooms and a large office with huge windows opening on to a grassy area were located on the lower level. During half a year in 1995, an intense drama would play out in that office, starring the tiny Dietrich Corporation and the U.S. Department of Energy (DOE).

and whether he was aware of any amounts bid by other companies. I would have asked these questions if we had had a chance to talk before his passing in 2009.

Crony capitalism I understand: Conoco and George Herbert Walker Bush, Enron and George W. Bush, Occidental Petroleum and Albert Gore Sr. and Jr., and a myriad of others. Until the U.S. Supreme Court overturns Citizens United, there will be no improvement. It was the unprecedented nasty nature of the IPE experience that was so disappointing, no where else encountered during my 50 years in the industry. It's as though public employees and those working on their behalf have a sense of entitlement. Apparently, others feel the same. In May 2013, the U.S. Court of Federal Claims ruled that Chevron USA is entitled to unspecified damages against the federal government, stating that, "The U.S. DOE repeatedly and materially violated two agreements governing determination of equity interests in the oil and gas deposits at Elk Hills." Furthermore, they ruled that, "Chevron is entitled to be compensated for damages, in an amount to be determined, including sanctions for the DOE and the government's bad faith conduct and abusive discovery tactics."

While at U.C. Berkeley, a required advanced class in my graduate curriculum was called Group Studies, taught by an adjunct professor employed by Bechtel Corporation, at that time the largest civil engineering company in the country with nuclear power plant construction at its core. This professor described his on-going field mapping work aimed at finding an alternative isthmian canal route to replace the Panama Canal, that was becoming too narrow for a new fleet of future, bigger ships. It was a fascinating course, with lots of photos showing the professor in his canoe in the jungles of Central America. As part of the course, I visited the Lawrence Berkeley National Laboratory (LBNL), just up the hill from the Berkeley campus, where later I would work as a consulting engineering geologist to help control a landslide that was threatening the facility, there to interview scientists who I learned were studying the use of nuclear explosives to excavate a new canal. I had wondered what kind of research public funds were supporting at LBNL!

Decades later, I was surprised to learn that the U.S. DOE was funding research aimed at recovering oil from diatomite at both the Lawrence Berkeley National Laboratory and Sandia Laboratories in Albuquerque, New Mexico. I thought these national labs were exclusively doing fundamental science and making contributions like mapping the universe, discovering dark energy and advancing superconductor technology. The focus of the publicly sponsored diatomite research was on the effect oil production was having on reservoir compaction and surface subsidence, the very same topic of my private consortium research project, the California Diatomite Thermal Study Project, that had concluded a year earlier. It dawned on me that I was paying competitors to compete with me! My corporate and personal taxes, and tax contributions from others in the private sector, were being used to fund the U.S. DOE and their national labs. It became clear that privately funded consortium research proposals would face a tough time getting accepted in the future. In no small part, it was the U.S. Department of Energy that kept me focusing on overseas contract employment as a consulting petroleum engineer. And that turned out to be a good thing.

CHAPTER SEVEN

IVAN THE WONDERFUL

Halfway through the Elk Hills project, I received a phone call from Ivan de Grisogono, who had moved within Germany from Wintershall AG to Deminex GmbH as the Chief Reservoir Engineer. He was calling from Essen, the headquarters of Deminex, and he wanted to meet there. It had been more than a decade since we had last talked, saying goodbye at the Folies Bergere on the last night of a conference in Paris. He collected me at the Dusseldorf airport and we drove to his home in Essen, sitting down for dinner immediately after being introduced to his boss, the Managing Director, their wives and the boss's German Shepherd. It was an important social event, unexpected and difficult after the long flight from California. The twinkle in Ivan's eye and his aforementioned sense of humor were missing, neither to return over the coming years of our renewed business relationship. The Bosnian War was coming to a close after nearly four years. I think it was the war that played-out in the backyard of his ancestral home that had changed him. As before, we never spoke of the break up of Yugoslavia.

I made it a point to give the Managing Director's dog some attention during the evening. A contract was cut the next day and I began work in Essen on a field development project of several reservoirs in Russia. The Russians wanted the Germans as a working interest owner, a partner to share the capital and operating costs of developing and operating the field. It was a question best answered by the application of reservoir simulation, "How fast might the oil come out and how much oil might ultimately be recovered?" There was lots of work and I would be in Essen for two months, a period of time when my associates could handle the Elk Hills work. The contract called for an all-in hourly rate, a single number that includes compensation for engineering man-time, local living expenses and health insurance. That billing model is ideal, since it removes the need to collect and submit receipts for taxi rides, meals, laundry, hotel rooms and the like, and it allows for compensation when working more than 8 hours per day. The contract allowed for invoicing an additional ½ of the man-time hourly rate for travel, plus reimbursement of airfares. Getting paid for putting up with all the annoyances of air travel was an element worth adding to the list during contract negotiation. The normal European invoicing model is on a daily rate basis, either including or excluding local living costs. It applies nearly everywhere in the world outside of North America. I checked into a hotel near the train station and walked about ¾ of a mile to work, benefitting from the exercise and avoiding a car rental at the same time. My desk was at one of two workstations in a 3rd floor computer room, which was bright and airy with operable windows that needed to be open. It must have been a real sweat shop with closed windows during the winter. On my first morning, a company engineer of British heritage opened the office door and upon entry said, "You know, we really don't want you here." That was unprecedented. I would later learn he was one of several company representatives of the European Works Council, a group formed as a response to increased transnational restructuring brought about by the Single European Act. As a non-European consultant, I was not subject to the same rules imposed on European employees, such as a requirement to work no more, and no less, than a certain number of hours per week. It was not rare to observe company employees sneaking back up the stairs to complete office work in the evenings, after punching out on the time clock in the lobby. I understood that it was galling for an employee to know HS (himself, or me) was being paid for each and every hour at the office and reporting directly to senior management. The Council representative was a portly fellow who clearly enjoyed drinking a lot of German beer, confirmed during my invitation for a long lunch taken that first day. After awhile, I felt less unwelcome.

Why was Ivan wonderful? It wasn't only because of all the work he brought our way. It was also because he handled all the office politics and made me an untouchable, meaning that he gave me full technical control of each project. When it came to building a model of a reservoir for simulation purposes, it was made clear to company specialists that I was the principal model architect. The models were built my way and I had full support from top management, presumably as a result of that successful dinner meeting with the Managing Director. Oh, how I would miss this bestowed authority during the later years of my consulting career! A power struggle was just beginning in the industry at that time for control of the reservoir modeling process, which is at the heart of determining the size of a company's hydrocarbon reserves and hence its value. The battle that has nearly played out now is between geologists and engineers. It's the subject of the final part of this book.

The Russian partner sent three of its top engineers to work with us for two weeks in Essen. They were all PhDs familiar with the project reservoirs and they brought data needed for building the models. They were of course technically very capable, but they were behind in the reservoir simulation technology that had its roots in Houston. The Schlumberger simulator was leased for the project, running on a Sun Microsystems, Inc. workstation, owned by Deminex. This was an epic change, marking the first time a foreign client company could afford to own computing equipment that was powerful enough to run simulations of reservoir performance. In prior years, as an international consulting petroleum engineer, I would gather the data while in the clients' offices and return to the United States to rent computer time on fast machines. Two or three progress meetings would take place during the project to keep everything running smoothly. With affordable powerful computing equipment came the requirement to work in the clients' offices for months at a time, where the benefits of collaborative effort could be realized. My wife, aka the trailing spouse (TS), joined me in Essen for most of the project, arriving a week later and returning a week earlier than myself, to set a pattern that would apply during the next two decades of our expat lives. I needed time to focus on a new project without distraction, and she preferred returning early to set up the home for our return. I would often be surprised upon my homecoming to view memorabilia for the first time, purchased surreptitiously, transported in her luggage and now mounted on the walls, covering the bed or bordering the windows. While reviewing each room after my long absence, I felt like Peter Sellers's Inspector Clouseau, expecting the houseboy Kato to jump out from hiding to attack while waving a surprise souvenir in his hands.

The Russians were on a tight budget for personal expenses and I recall that clean laundry became an issue after the first week. There was good companionship and a few dinners for all project members at long tables along the Ruhr riverside, with strings of party lights overhead, not far from Villa Huegel, the family home of Krupp, and the heart of the prodigious German munitions factories. It was all very eerie at times. I wrote a final report and returned to California, where I continued working on the Elk Hills equity dispute.

I returned to Essen the following summer to continue working on the same project, this time for a period of 3 months. The night the TS arrived, the Germans had just won the 1996 UEFA European Football Championship, a quadrennial football tournament contested by European nations. The hotel was circled by slowly moving automobiles with their horns honking throughout the night in celebration, preventing the possibility of sleep. The

TS found Schloss Lembeck the next day, a place that was to become our home that summer and also in later years when on business in Essen. It's a moated 17th century baroque castle with about a dozen rooms for rent, located 25 minutes north of Essen by rental car. It was built by Conrad Dietrich von Westholt-Hackfurt and owned by the same family for the last 300 years. We paid a nightly rate that was less than an average hotel price in Essen. And even when wedding parties booked the place for a weekend, a room was always made available for us. On weekends we enjoyed entertaining clients from Deminex, sharing sparkling wine in our large rooms and meals along the moat. Perhaps as with Mirabell Palace, it was our family name that got us the special treatment. It got to where we just went up to our room after finishing dinner, without needing to wait for a bill to sign or pay, knowing that the German record keeping would be correct at settlement time. Avoiding that daily tedium was priceless.

It was the drilling of new wells into the project reservoirs that had brought us back to Essen. A better understanding of the reservoir geometry was now in-hand and it was time to update the reservoir models. Prior to using a reservoir simulator to predict reservoir performance, it must first be adjusted or tuned to match historical reservoir performance. There will always be some history that gives important information, even if it's just the fluid saturation profile or pressure determined in a well that was a dry hole. When taking this standard modeling step, I found it was not possible to reproduce the low pressure gradients measured in the project reservoirs using the models prepared by the project geologists. There was no reasonable way to match the historical gradients without modeling better pore-space connectivity, where pore space is simply the part of a permeable rock that contains oil and other fluids. The subject reservoirs are called pinnacle reefs and a technical paper had recently been published on this type of reservoir by a distinguished petroleum engineer. He described the same problem I was facing and a solution for it, a solution that called for a different approach than that being used in the industry.

Geologists had recently settled on a technique introduced in the mining industry decades earlier called geostatistics as the norm for distributing pore space and other rock properties within a reservoir model. There is a basic assumption in geostatistics that geological properties may be regarded as regionalized variables — variables that are distributed in space and have an underlying structure or organization within their apparent irregularity, where the measure of this underlying structure is called a proximity function. Acceptance of this key assumption opened the door for mathematicians and statisticians to develop the discipline of geostatistics for probability modeling of reservoir property distributions. Complex and very expensive geostatistics computer programs are owned by only a handful of companies, with the industry giants Schlumberger and Halliburton Energy Services having most of the market share. These programs are either leased or perpetually licensed to hundreds of companies who use reservoir simulation technology. They are separate from the simulator itself — pre-processing programs simply set up the data for entry into the simulator and post-processing programs display the computed results as a series of static images or in full animation, with a quality that approaches that provided to movie-goers by Pixar Animation Studios. A major oil company requires multiple licenses and maintenance agreements for this software, each renewed and paid on an annual basis. Even a single license is prohibitive for most small energy firms.

As an alternative to the use of geostatistical methods, detailed distributions of reservoir properties may be constructed by drawing random numbers from a population having the same mean and variance as the property being simulated and assigning them to locations with no regard for the values of neighboring points. In this approach, the presence of spatial correlations in properties is completely ignored. In that key publication on pinnacle reef reservoirs, reservoir properties had been distributed manually using a random number generator, allowing good pore-space connectivity and reproduction of the measured pressure gradients. I commissioned an expert programmer to write a computer program to distribute reservoir properties using this conditioned random distribution procedure in a manner that allowed the property arrays to be directly inserted into the commercially available reservoir simulators. This solution approach quickly gave good results when applied to the project reservoirs, and it would be a technique used for every project over the next two decades where I was given authority to use it.

Deminex asked that I visit the Russians in Volgograd (renamed from Stalingrad) to evaluate their reservoir simulation work on the project reservoirs. I was scheduled to fly from Dusseldorf to Frankfurt where I was to meet the project geologist for a connecting flight to Volgograd. When landing in Frankfurt, a tire blew-out. The pilot was unable to keep the aircraft on the runway and planted its nose wheel in soft ground, causing me to miss my connection. I flew the next day non-stop from Dusseldorf to Moscow and then on to Volgograd, traveling solo for my first entry into Russia. As an experienced traveler it was nonetheless difficult with all signage in the Cyrillic Russian alphabet. A one hour taxi ride was needed to transfer from the international to the domestic airport in Moscow, where one could barely see through the grime on the windows in the gate area and the toilets were unusable. It was a new sight to see passengers standing in the aisle gathering their items from overhead when the plane was landing in Volgograd and still hundreds of feet above the runway. I recall pounding on the locked door of the hotel upon arriving after midnight to rouse a guard sleeping on a cot in the lobby. There was a bare light bulb hanging from the ceiling on its electrical cord and rust trails coated the porcelain fixtures in the bathroom. Homeless groups of men and women talked throughout the night in a park across the street, heard through windows that remained open due to the heat. The project geologist from Essen who had arrived the prior day was from the former East Germany and had graduated from Moscow University. When having dinner together in Volgograd after our meeting with the Russians, we were approached by an elderly woman who asked for money. My colleague gladly obliged and I followed in form. He was not pleased with the results of Perestroika, the supposed restructuring of the economy that had been introduced a decade earlier — there were now many more people asking for help and sleeping in the public parks.

The meeting confirmed my views that the Russians certainly didn't want or need our technical expertise. They quickly understood and applied reservoir simulation technology. In later years, during four separate contracts in Moscow for different companies, I came to understand what it was the Russians wanted from the West, particularly from American oil men. Mostly British, Dutch and German companies provided the funds and services needed for field development. American consulting engineers were in high demand to provide project management skills that were utterly missing from the centrally planned Russian economy. After hearing the technical presentation given by the Russians and reacting favorably to it, we all adjourned to an adjacent room where a senior official unlocked a cabinet and removed several bottles of vodka. It was early afternoon. I had expected this and was ready with two separate toasts, each given when it became my consecutive turn to say something nice, and preferably humorous, upon doing bottoms-up. I do recall not being prepared for the third round.

While in Volgograd for that business meeting, I realized that Deminex drilling engineers and geophysicists had been working there for more than a year, evaluating whether to partner with the Russians on a number of business opportunities. There seemed to be no enmity between the two groups, notwithstanding the carnage suffered by the Russian people in the legendary, bloody siege of Stalingrad during WWII. I would later observe the same benign behavior between Germans and Russians in Moscow, bringing to mind the adage that half a century can settle most anything.

Upon my return to Essen, I began writing the project report, after the TS had returned to California to reopen our home. The key result coming from reservoir simulation was the awareness that wells needed to be drilled quickly on undeveloped acreage to reduce the drainage of oil already occurring to offsetting properties that had been developed by competitors. The Schloss was a creepy place to sleep alone. There was little outside lighting and the oak plank flooring made groaning and creaking sounds during the night as the hotel staff pursued their tasks and the few guests came and went. I recall hoards of bats at dusk, circling above the moat feeding on myriads of insects, screeching as they passed my small windows that were open for ventilation and without screens. I would soon learn that my next contract with Deminex would take us to Oslo, Norway, a location where dwindling colonies of bats struggle under the midnight sun.

CHAPTER EIGHT

ADJUNCT TO STAFF

The Snorre oil field is located beneath the North Sea, about 90 miles offshore from the west coast of Norway. It began first production in 1992, initially with ten owning companies, including Deminex Norge AS with a 10% non-operating share. The original equity split was due for redetermination, a standard procedure that is followed when development drilling provides new information about how the oil-in-place is distributed among the different ownership areas. Prior to leaving for Volgograd, I had approached Deminex management and provided a written proposal to them, describing how evaluation of an EOR process in the subject reservoir might yield a result that would support raising their equity share. The EOR process was the alternating injection of a miscible hydrocarbon gas and water (called an MWAG procedure), known to be capable of increasing oil recovery as compared to water injection only. The efficiency of the MWAG process is dependent on the geological properties of the individual zones within the reservoir. And since the rules for determining equity share were based in part on zone recovery factors, it made sense to evaluate the option. Snorre is a major field, with about 3.2 billion barrels of initial oil-in-place. Even a fraction of an equity percentage point was worth tens of millions of dollars on a present value basis. What's called a compositional reservoir simulator is needed for evaluation of MWAG, and the team already in place in Oslo had little, or no, experience with evaluation of EOR processes. The team was composed of British and Norwegian consultants, reporting to the project director, who was a Deminex employee and an Austrian. A Norwegian petroleum engineer served as a subsurface project manager.

After returning home, I learned that the Deminex Board of Directors had approved my proposal, which called for working on the project in California. I bought a powerful Silicon Graphics workstation for $27,000, leased the Schlumberger compositional simulator and began building a geological model of the reservoir. After several months, when the simulator had been tuned by reproducing key laboratory test results and was running at the field scale, I was asked to proceed with the project in Oslo. This was a pleasant surprise, as springtime was approaching and we had not previously lived in Norway. The client agreed to modify the contract to cover a few issues related to the change of work location. Additional funds were needed for reimbursement of local living expenses and to ship my computer to and from Oslo. Living expenses for this contract and all future ones were covered by a negotiated per-diem, where the daily dollar-equivalent number was calculated using an average 21 work days per month, not the number of calendar days in a month. One needed to cover expenses on the weekends and holidays when the office was closed. In our case, we simply wanted to cover all out-of-pocket expenses related to doing business, without a mark-up. Local expenses typically included housing, meals, transportation and laundry. All health insurance costs were on our own account. Regardless of where in the world a contract was written, we insisted on the option of handling our own housing. The client requested that we stay by the month in their arranged company housing. We gave it a try and quickly activated our option, as the property was filled with stressed young families moving into and out of Oslo. We often increased the approved housing budget with funds of our own to live comfortably on our expat assignments. This was the only contract where my computer was needed on-site. Compositional simulation requires a much more powerful machine than a normal black-oil simulation and the client was not prepared for this necessity. I recall insisting that my equipment could not be networked with other computers for security reasons and that was agreed.

The technical approach that had been proposed and accepted in the contract called for simulating the MWAG process in a series of reservoir models, progressing in complexity from one to two-dimensional models and ending with three-dimensional models of the reservoir. In compositional simulation, this type of progression must be followed to build an understanding of the oil recovery mechanisms that vary from one reservoir application to another. The necessary procedures were established and published as best practice in North America during the heyday of enhanced oil recovery, an era that had come and gone as oil prices had risen and fallen during the late 1970s and early 1980s. EOR processes had generally not been applied in Europe during the period of high oil prices because the field developments were younger there and not yet ready for EOR. No wonder the Norwegian and British team members lobbied the project director to stop my independent work and reassign tasks to me that fit into a technical approach they knew. This Norwegian project marked the first time I was asked to work as an adjunct to staff, led by others and not allowed to perform as an independent consultant. In every prior project, I was given full control of the technical work flow.

The attempt to change my assignment came in the form of a 2-hour meeting, called at the end of my first week in Oslo. When listening to the clarion call for my redirection, I was keen to understand the motivation for it. It was mostly coming from a Norwegian consultant who had helped build the reservoir model in use by SAGA Petroleum AS, the operator of Snorre. That model may have been suitable for evaluation of water injection processes, but it was much too coarse for compositional simulation. No matter how bright an engineer, I found that if he thought he already understood the technical issues involved with a new subject, it was not possible to bring him on board with the accepted best practice procedures. There also seemed to be a sense of nationalism underlying the mind-sets of both the Norwegian and British consultants. Not only was an American taking a consulting position from one of their compatriots in their own back yard, but each of their own countries had more Nobel laureates than almost any other. Why would they need to look elsewhere for understanding a new technology?

All this prompted me to write a brief letter to the project director, stating that I was unable to accept the modified work plan prepared by the Norwegian consultant, and to let me know in writing if it was not acceptable for me to proceed with the scope of work outlined in my contract. Per the rules of the equity redetermination process, an expert was to be brought in to review the technical work underlying an owner's claimed equity share. My position was simple: I had a lot of EOR experience and other team members did not. I was following a technical course that would hopefully hold-up under its review by an expert. In the absence of a response, I finished my scope of work and wrote a project report during the next two months, while in an office environment that was a little less than friendly. The office was located in the suburb of Lysaker, about a 2 mile walk from our hotel in the center of Oslo. It was cold but pleasant when walking briskly to work along a route that passed the Aker Brygge Marina, where in the evenings owners of wooden boats were busy removing old layers of varnish and applying new ones. The overall experience in Oslo was a good one. We enjoyed dinners in cozy restaurants with welcoming, glowing candles at the entrances labeling them as open, and a few weekend trips were taken by train to visit Bergen and several fjords.

I participated in a 2-day retreat planned by the project director, at a resort reached after driving about 2 hours from Oslo. It was attended by the entire team of about 20 Deminex Norge staff and consultants. In a small group of us sitting at a lakeside table one evening, the project director uttered an anti-Semitic remark and actually revealed himself to be a holocaust inverter, stating that what happened to the Jews was highly exaggerated. I had rarely heard these types of comments, never while in a public setting. At the time, no one reacted and I assumed it was simply the view of a lone Austrian. Later I learned that Norway is a European leader of anti-Semitic cartoons. Major anti-Semitic incidents had recently taken place there, and in other Nordic countries. The project director must have felt emboldened to publicly express such polarizing views, aided that evening by a schnapps or two.

During our first week in Oslo, we were surprised by the number of parties happening not only on the weekends but on any night of the week. They were high energy events, with loud music, in full celebration mode and often running till dawn. While at the office with deadlines looming, I would see workers appear and then be gone for a day or more, whenever the sun was shining. I would later understand that it was springtime, a time to rejoice after the long, dark winter. And then the ability to relax and have fun may also have had a basis in the huge economic safety net that is beneath each and every Norwegian. The Sovereign Wealth Fund of Norway administers the oil profits. It is the largest of any country at 900 billion dollars, ahead of those of Saudi Arabia and the United Arab Emirates. After inflation and management fees, the fund had been generating roughly 35 billion dollars annually. Investments are highly diversified with prime London and New York City real estate recently added to the mix. It's a government pension fund, meaning that with a population of only 5.2 million, each Norwegian's share is presently worth ~ 175,000 dollars. It only gets better for a Norwegian. The Johan Sverdrup oil field was discovered offshore Norway in the year 2010. It's enormous, bigger than Snorre and expected to come on stream in the year 2019. Helping to understand its size and potential marked the penultimate project of my business life (Chapter 22).

CHAPTER NINE

IMPLODING CAIRO

Within two months of completing the contract in Oslo, we were living in a Marriott Hotel in the center of Cairo, working on the Zeit Bay oil field under a new contract with Deminex. Zeit Bay is located on the Gulf of Suez in Egypt. It was operated by Suez Oil Company (SUCO), a joint venture at the time between Deminex Egypt Branch and the Egyptian General Petroleum Corporation. The oil reservoirs in Egypt are small as compared to those offshore Norway and scattered throughout the country, in the Western and Eastern Deserts, the Sinai and near the Suez Canal. Zeit Bay was discovered in 1981 and it came on stream in 1984. I was being retained to predict how much more oil was likely to be produced after 1998, using reservoir simulation technology. Unknown to me and others at the time, Deminex was going to be broken up and sold the following year to RWE-DEA of Hamburg and Veba AG of Dusseldorf. The planned sale had been kept very quiet. It was only after the sale that I understood why I had been asked to help with establishing the Norwegian and Egyptian oil reserves of Deminex.

On the first day of work I reported to the project manager at the ground floor entrance to the SUCO building. He was a seasoned British petroleum engineer, who had recently taken the position in Cairo and was clearly pleased to have another expat on board. He had a twinkle in his eye and a quick sense of humor that was appreciated after my recent stint in Oslo. The office was located on the 14th floor, and I was given the option of either walking up the stairs or taking a very slow and crowded elevator. It was July and hot and the stairs were not easy, given that I was carrying personal items and a heavy laptop computer. How could HS decline to participate in what seemed to be a challenging initiation test? Arriving in my office shared with three Egyptian engineers, one of them said, "You look much older than the picture we were given." There was a full roll of toilet paper on my desk that may have been taken as an insult, until glancing at other desks of both men and women showed that all desks were similarly adorned. It was later learned that a new roll was placed on each desk at the beginning of each week. Next I was introduced to Ahmed, who had an office to himself and the same managing position as the Brit, but for a different group of oil fields. This was my first time in a Muslim country and in the next few minutes a lot that was different came my way. I stepped away from Ahmed's office for a moment and into the men's room, where urinals were absent and the floors were covered with water. The Egyptian male clothing standard is a full-length robe called a gallibaya, a garment that does not really work with a urinal. And then it was soon understood that washing feet before prayer left the bathroom floors wet and slippery throughout the day. Upon my return, Ahmed was no where to be seen — he had hit the floor behind his large desk to pray for the second time that morning.

Zeit Bay is unusual because its wells produce not only from the normal sandstone and carbonate rock types, but also from fractured igneous rock. It was recognized from the start that building a reasonable reservoir model of the complex geology was going to be a challenge. Although the Brit and myself were given freedom to develop the work program, it soon became apparent that we had no control over the Egyptian project geologists. We were able to describe what was needed and when, but that was about it. This project marked the first time I was not able to control the modeling process.

Previously, projects of this nature had either been outsourced to consulting firms like Todd, Dietrich & Chase, or The Dietrich Corporation, or Ivan had quietly taken care of any problems within Deminex in Essen. The Egyptian geologists had access to the powerful earth modeling software that was new and commercially available from Schlumberger and Halliburton. They were learning how to use it and wanted to work independently, at their own pace. After several months when little progress had been made on building the reservoir model, the Brit and I made a recommendation to outsource the work to experts in either the United Kingdom or America. It was explained that this was not possible because it would leave the local staff with nothing to do. When arriving for work in the mornings, I would see a long queue of busses unloading hoards of SUCO staff, a sight that once again brought the unvoiced question to mind, "How many people can an oil field support?"

Our hotel had been built in 1869 as a palace for the Viceroy of Egypt and Sudan, a man who greatly modernized the country and expanded its boundaries, yet whose policies left Egypt in so much debt that it was forced to sell its shares in the Suez Canal to the British. Marriott International purchased the property and upgraded the palace, leaving it in place to connect two identical 19-story towers, newly built to house the hotel guest rooms, each with a balcony and a view of downtown Cairo.

There were several restaurants, located both inside and outside, all with marble floors, fountains and beautiful plantings everywhere. It was for the most part a very comfortable accommodation during the 6-month contract. However, Cairo to a Muslim from Saudi Arabia or the United Arab Emirates is like Las Vegas to a Mormon from Utah. The hotel with its casino was a big draw on Arabian Gulf Arabs, who would arrive to take over an entire floor of the hotel, letting their children run up and down the halls from one family guest room to another, with entry doors wide open, while the men were gambling and carousing throughout the night. Although Egyptians speak a form of Arabic and most are Sunni Muslims, they are not Arabs. The Egyptian Human Rights Organization periodically reports abuse, exploitation and/or ill treatment of Egyptian workers and professionals employed in the Arab states of the Arabian Gulf, where those holding petrodollars are the masters. While relaxing in one of the courtyards at the Marriott, it was not uncommon to witness a Gulf Arab simply tossing the remnants of an unwanted beverage over his shoulder, onto the marble floor, and then following with a summons for the hotel staff to wipe it up.

Why Imploding Cairo? My sense upon arrival in the city was that the life style was not sustainable, a premonition born out by the revolution that would take place a decade and a half later. It was all too complex, people seemed to be annoyed, living on the edge, relying on foreign aid and an uneven stream of tourist revenue that comes and goes, depending on the level of terrorist activity. It's the rapidly growing population, a limitation of arable land, political repression, human rights violations by Egypt's ruling regimes, corruption and little opportunity for economic growth that all underlay, and still underlie, the feeling that Cairo was going to implode and will again. On the run up to the revolution and Mubarak's exodus in 2011, the economic situation in Egypt had only worsened. The country became a net oil importer in 2008 for the first time and is approaching the same status as a net importer of natural gas, resulting in reduced government funding available for domestic infrastructure and social welfare programs. Energy conservation is critical. Maintenance that requires a shut-down of a factory or facility is now purposely scheduled during the summer, when the burning of natural gas as a fuel source is at its peak.

When nearing the end of the contract and without receiving a reservoir model from the SUCO geologists, I was asked to review and update an old model, so that we could move forward with simulating reservoir performance. Although data from recently drilled wells were missing from the model, encouraging results were obtained and there was a positive feel about the project at the end of the contract. The Zeit Bay oil reservoir is termed a 3-phase system, meaning oil, water and natural gas were all present as separate phases when the reservoir was discovered. An initial band of oil was overlain by a primary gas cap and underlain by water in an aquifer, like a sandwich with oil in the middle of the system. When simulating the historical performance, it was found that the thickness of the oil band was shrinking less rapidly than expected, meaning more oil would ultimately come out of this reservoir than all had projected. A process called *surface film drainage* had been described by a researcher at Esso Production Research, a process known to occur in some but not all reservoirs, leading to high oil recovery under the right conditions. The response from logging tools run in the wells at Zeit Bay established that oil was indeed draining upward to replenish the oil band, ostensibly in a surface film drainage process. After adjusting the physics entered into the simulator, it was shown to be capable of reproducing the upward drainage of oil owing to buoyancy forces, long after passage of a water front from the invading aquifer. This initial tuning step was necessary prior to generating a series of predictive simulations that each showed the likelihood of recovering more oil than ever anticipated. All this was presented to an interested staff and carefully documented in the final project report. Although the reservoir model was deficient, the project ending was satisfactory.

CHAPTER TEN

CAESAR SALAD DINNER

In October 2000, I was under contract with Schlumberger in Moscow, where I was seconded to Yukos Oil Corporation. Yukos owned and operated a number of huge oil fields and was producing 20% of Russia's total oil output between 1996 and 2003, as much oil as produced by either Libya or Iraq. Its assets had been acquired from the Russian government by Bank Menatep, owned by a 32-year old Russian oligarch, Mikhail Khodorkovsky, during the controversial loans for shares auctions during the mid 1990s. At the time, Khodorkovsky was said to be the wealthiest man in Russia and number 16 on the global list of billionaires.

After Cairo, we needed a break from international travel and our quiet adobe home in the Santa Ynez Valley of California was the perfect sanctuary. It was built during the period from 1882-1884 and positioned on an acre of land with many majestic oaks and olive trees.

While working at home on consulting projects for the City of Long Beach and Shell Canada, a colleague called to say he was passing through on his drive home to Santa Cruz, not far up the California coast. We had worked together at Intercomp in Houston and had not been in touch for two decades. He was returning to the United States after living in Moscow, where he had opened an office for Occidental Petroleum. We shared a few tales of

Russia while sitting on the back porch of the Adobe, looking out on acres of beautiful vineyards.

Why a contract with Schlumberger? As arguably the premier oilfield services company in the world, Schlumberger had gained an early entrance into Russia in 1998, when it was the first to set up a series of collaborative research projects with Russian universities at a Schlumberger-Moscow Research Center. An American, Joe Mach, had earned a reputation for getting the highest possible production rate out of an oil well, first at Gulf Oil Corporation and then at Schlumberger. He is to an oil well as a horse whisperer is to a horse. While at Schlumberger in Moscow, Mach had recognized that the steady decline in the Russian oil production rate, including that at Yukos, was due in large part to how the wells were being operated. He recognized that many of the pumps needed to be resized and set much lower in the wellbores. This was a different strategy that was much less capital intensive than drilling nearly a thousand wells a year, a practice that had been routinely followed by Yukos. His initiative to enhance production through operations rather than drilling was understood and interesting to the CEO, Khodorkovsky, who hired Mach away from Schlumberger, giving him the title of Senior VP of Production and a seat next to him on the corporate jet. There was a second major reason for declining oil production, easily recognizable to a petroleum engineer trained in North America. Nearly all oil fields in Russia are under waterflood, meaning that water is injected into injection wells to support the reservoir pressure and sweep oil to production wells. The production and injection wells need to be drilled in regular geometrical patterns to prevent early water breakthrough to a production well and loss of oil reserves. The Russians had not done a good job laying out the necessary patterns and, given early water breakthrough, they simply continued to cycle water between an injector and a producer, producing very little oil in the process. It took a lot of courage in a state-run system to shut-in a well that was producing even a little oil, because it would take months, or longer, for that previously cycled water to redistribute itself and push out more oil from un-swept areas of the reservoir. Recognizing that a reservoir management expert was needed, Mach hired a prior colleague away from Schlumberger in the United States by the name of Don Wolcott. With a PhD in petroleum engineering from the Colorado School of Mines, Wolcott had worked in research for Arco. Mach and Wolcott were undertaking a massive effort, with 15,000 wells in the Yukos roster and a bevy of young Russian university graduates to train, only half of whom had majored in STEM subjects.

While we were visiting at the Adobe, my colleague asked if I might be available to work in Moscow for Schlumberger, who was seconding consultants to Yukos on a regular basis. Unknown at the time, that introduction would lead to several different contracts in Moscow during the following four years. Arriving a week earlier than my trailing spouse (TS), I was required to attend a series of films at Schlumberger on my first day, where I was made aware that the use of drugs, driving under the influence, or riding in a company vehicle or taxi without a seat belt in-place was grounds for immediate dismissal. As a contractor rather than an employee, there was no information provided about the need to register with the U.S. Embassy, the areas of Moscow to be avoided, emergency contact numbers or what to do given the need for medical assistance. For legal reasons, the big company needed to remain at arms length from its contractors. We liked it that way! The challenge was exciting. Just give us the money and stay out of our way. I reported to Wolcott, who held the position of VP of Production. He reported to no others than Mach and Khodorkovsky. A bright, very aggressive personality, he could be amusing and loved center stage, always seeking to be the most charismatic person in the room. One had the sense he was on a fortune hunt in Moscow, leaving his family ranching background in Wyoming, never to return. To remain in Russia, learn the language and replace his American wife with a Russian one were seemingly all part of the script. He was fully committed to his new life and he had to be — it was tough to be an American boss in Russia, an impossible challenge without the full support and autocratic authority prearranged by Khodorkovsky.

The job description in my contract was explicit. I was to lead a team of Russians to evaluate the reserves and productive capacity of the Yurubcheno-Tokhomskoye (Y-T) oil field, located 2,500 miles east of Moscow and under license to the East Siberian Oil and Gas Company, at the time a subsidiary of Yukos. Oil exports from Yukos to China were rapidly growing and Khodorkovsky had decided to establish his own production base in East Siberia, building a private pipeline to move oil into Daqing, in northeast China. It was claimed that the Y-T field alone was big enough to supply the planned pipeline and justify its construction. Three young men were assigned to my team and each was a model of the diverse ethnic groups that make up the Russian Federation: Iskander is a mathematician, lean with patrician features; Rushan is a production or development geologist, with strong Asian features; and Konstantin is a mechanical engineer, with the thick, powerful body of a Boris Yeltsin. The first two were fluent in English and they translated for Konstantin when he had something to say. My impression from the start was that they were terrific in technical capability and attitude, ahead of most other young colleagues in the industry. That sense was unchanging throughout the duration of the project and remains so today.

I had chosen the Savoy Hotel, not far from the Bolshoi Theatre, in the center of Moscow as our temporary home. Arrival of the trailing spouse (TS) marked her first time in Russia and I knew she would be pleased with my selection. Our hotel room had high ceilings and it was a corner room on the second floor, looking onto a quiet street. The price including an unbelievable breakfast and taxes was the equivalent of 3,800 dollars monthly. Now it's a 5-star hotel and unaffordable for a long-term stay. Colleagues we would later meet worked for BP, Caterpillar, ConocoPhillips, Ernst and Young, Halliburton, Philip Morris, Shell or UBS. Their jobs in Moscow typically ran between 2 to 4 years and their monthly housing costs varied between 12,000 to 22,000 dollars. We found it amusing that the Russian property management companies knew, and charged, exactly the price authorized by the HR Department of each company for employee housing. These big company people would arrive with one or two shipping containers filled with furniture, household goods and personal effects, each measuring about 8 feet by 9 feet by 40 feet, often for only the employee and trailing spouse. And then a cat or dog also usually came with the package.

We loved our exciting yet simple life style. On our first night together in Moscow, we happily went to dinner around the corner from the Savoy, at a Mexican restaurant across the street from the prior headquarters of the KGB. As usual, the TS had done her research before arriving and called attention to the previously unseen and important building. The restaurant was unique, with an ebony skinned woman passing from table to table, wearing double holsters on her hips that held bottles of vodka and tequila instead of a pair of six-guns. There were many good restaurants offering international food choices, but we noticed they would come and go. It was rumored the failing ones had tax compliance issues with the Kremlin and our transitory Mexican restaurant was supposedly one of them. Taking a drink in the bar at the Savoy was an event, for the open mezzanine was a frequent meeting place reserved for business where a young, athletic bodyguard dressed in an expensive suit would be seated alone, just out of hearing range from his boss, the outline of a weapon exposed through his clothing.

> We are pleased to announce
> the formation of *Todd, Dietrich & Chase,*
> a firm offering professional
> reservoir engineering services with
> particular emphasis on numerical simulation
> and enhanced oil recovery.
>
> Reservoir Engineering · Thermal Processes
> Enhanced Recovery · Numerical Reservoir Simulation
> 2111 Briarcrest, Houston, Texas 77077 (713) 493-3025
>
> Todd, Dietrich & Chase

1. The consultancy of TDC was formed in January 1979, one of the earliest firms offering numerical reservoir simulation software and services.

2. The opening page of Roger Parsons' website http://iran-conoco-affair. us., where a massive government/corporate cover-up of an air disaster is described which tragically claimed the lives of his wife, the author's brother and sister-in-law and nine other persons. It's an incredible read.

3. The beautiful Mirabelle Gardens in Salzburg, Austria, was the location of the nuptials before the author and the TS began two decades of global petroleum consulting adventures.

4. Our carriage house rental in Santa Barbara was beautiful, but it was termite invested and held only negative equity for the owner. The DOE-Chevron equity dispute at the Elk Hills Naval Petroleum Reserve was sorted-out in the ground-floor office.

5. A rented room in Schloss Lembeck was usually our home when working in Essen, Germany.

6. The entrance to Schloss Lembeck, located about 20 miles north of Essen, Germany.

7. Enjoying an aperitif with Steve Baker in necktie, an American and graduate of Texas A&M, prior to his departure for Cairo, as Production Manager for Deminex.

8. Sunday afternoon in our room with Jim and Else Fuller
and John and Geraldine Rose, Brits who had worked for Schlumberger
before joining Deminex.

9. Evening meals along the moat were somehow
bug-free and truly incredible.

10. The windows had no screens and hoards of bats taking insects off the moat would endlessly circle and screech at nightfall.

11. Cairo Marriott Hotel located on Gezira Island situated on the Nile.

12. Courtyard with the "just-wipe-it-up" marble floors at the Cairo Marriott Hotel.

13. The Haynes Adobe in 2003, our sanctuary enjoyed while we were not living the expat life.

14. The Haynes Adobe in 1882-1884, built by the Haynes brothers,
who are viewed standing on the back porch.

15. Hotel Savoy in the center of Moscow, near the KGB Building and the
Bolshoi Theater, was our home in 2003 while working for Yukos.

16. The open mezzanine above the lobby bar at Hotel Savoy was reserved for Russian businessmen and their body guards.

This openness to an underworld is still a standard sight in Russia, not at the luxury hotels of the West, but at the European or Russian owned 5-star properties where management looks the other way for the right customers. Counterparts of signs on the entrance doors of diners in West Texas that say, "Leave your firearms in your truck," were missing in Moscow. "Blue light boys" was my label for those Russians who paid the right official for a blue light that was magnetically mounted on the roof of their always black BMW or Mercedes, allowing them to drive on the sidewalks around stopped traffic or in lanes of on-coming traffic while ignored by police. This entitled breed may be extinct now, as it was rumored at the time that groups of annoyed, young Russians were beginning to block at intersections, when possible, and literally overturn blue-light vehicles with their occupants in them. The rule for any expat driving in Moscow was to be assertive, not hesitant about his course. To do otherwise was to be recognized as a likely foreigner and quickly stopped by police, requiring the payment of an on-the-spot bribe before being allowed to continue with travel.

The office was a 15-minute commute via the underground metro system, with the nearest station only a walk of several blocks from the Savoy. During the winter, ice on the sidewalks was treacherous, requiring the elderly or infirm to actually crawl or strap crampons on their boots. I learned the hard way to step around areas of the sidewalk where downspouts drained water from rooftops that morphed into clear ice at night, waiting to take down the newly arrived foreigner on his early morning walk to the metro station. Escalators running at two to three times the speed of their North American or European counterparts transported passengers from the surface to the commuter trains two hundred feet below street level, in a system which was purposely built deep enough to serve as a massive bomb shelter. Street traffic does not move during the commuting hours and, for this reason, Moscow is known as one of the most difficult locations in the world for conducting business. Expats living outside of the city routinely leave their driver and vehicle to transfer to the metro when they reach a convenient station. A car and driver were not offered under our contract and they were not wanted. I recall being unable to get to work when one or more of the trains failed to appear at the normal 90-second intervals. When that occurred, hundreds of commuters would slowly converge on each narrow entrance of the two available escalators, requiring one to stand with arms at his side, pressed tightly all around by a mass of humanity. It was claustrophobic and I was psychologically incapable of it, proven one morning by the need to permanently leave the sluggishly moving queue after two false starts. I did better crossing the major streets that are three or four lanes wide, after learning to walk in the direction of the slow moving traffic, moving over a lane at a time in a zigzag manner.

Yukos was one of the first vertically integrated Russian oil companies to become interested in the East of Russia and to develop a long-term strategy for the region. Their main producing fields were located in West Siberia as were those of most other energy companies. The climate is more severe in the East and it has little transportation infrastructure. The few roads are only usable during the winter months when the permafrost is frozen. The Y-T field had been drilled by dozens of exploratory wells over several decades, each cored and tested to establish productive capacity. Small volumes of oil are produced from a few wells to fire boilers for local heating in the small, nearby villages. A group of research scientists has been studying the field continuously for decades, headed then and now by Alexi Kontorovich, a member of the Russian Academy of Sciences and a strong advocate of a tremendous productive capacity for the Y-T field and the entire East of Russia region. My team had access to massive amounts of data that were brought to Moscow by Kontorovich. It quickly became clear that reservoir simulation technology had not been used in prior evaluations and, in fact, that is why I had been retained for the project. The young Russians quickly absorbed all that I could teach them about reservoir simulation, studying the software manuals after hours until they were experts with the processing of data needed to build a series of reservoir models and view the computed results in a series of 3D images.

The geology of the field is complex, and like Zeit Bay it's a 3-phase system with a primary gas cap overlying a column of oil that in-turn is underlain by an aquifer. Some of the exploratory wells had produced at high oil rates that were commercial even under much lower oil prices. But others produced little oil or nothing at all. The good wells were clustered together in a small area where the tight carbonate rock was thought to have been naturally fractured. The research scientists of the East Siberia Oil and Gas Company had described fractures in the cores taken from many exploratory wells, including those that had produced no fluids. They interpreted these as natural fractures that had been filled with drilling mud and damaged during drilling, to such an extent that they were no longer capable of providing productive capacity. In some wells fractures were absent altogether, raising a question about the connectivity of the productive areas of the reservoir. There was a second major problem. Wells drilled to develop Y-T would need to be produced at rates much lower than their capacities in areas where the extensive gas cap is present. Where gas overlies oil, an oil well that is produced at higher rates than what is called the critical rate will become a gas well. In this situation, it becomes impossible to choke back the gas that moves downward into the oil column when a well is produced above the critical rate. The exploratory wells were tested for only short periods of time and they failed to highlight this limitation. While home in California for the Holiday Season, I completed some simulations on my Silicon Graphics workstation and checked the results. I concluded the Y-T field was incapable of filling more than a third of the pipeline capacity. More needed to be done before proceeding with the decision to build a pipeline running 1,500 miles to Daqing, China for a cost of 2 billion dollars, or more. I called Wolcott with the news before making my return to Moscow.

Of course there were a series of intense meetings upon my return, in which two actions were decided in an attempt to keep the project alive. The first was to bring in an expert in natural fracturing who had worked with Wolcott at Arco Research in Dallas, Texas. Our team had viewed photographs of core material and concluded that what were interpreted as damaged natural fractures by the Russian scientists were, instead, simply fractures that were caused by the coring process. The expert traveled to Krasnoyarsk in Eastern Siberia where the Y-T core material was in storage and confirmed upon his evaluation that, indeed, fractures in the wells that had produced little fluid were induced by stress release from the drilling and coring operations. They were not naturally formed and therefore they were limited in areal extent to the immediate regions of the drilled wells, implying that pore-space connectivity of the reservoir would be poor and unpredictable. Kontorovich pushed back strongly on this conclusion, leading Mach to decide a second action to resolve the issue. He moved two work-over rigs into the field that would be used to test the claim of the Russian scientists that the poor wells were good wells that had simply been damaged by the drilling and completion operations. Work-over rigs are smaller, less expensive to operate and more easily movable than a drilling rig. In this case, two of them would be moved from one poor well to another to remove the purported damage by pumping acid and re-perforating the steel casing in an attempt to get the well to produce. Alas, after months of effort this type of remedial activity failed to turn a poor well into a good one.

Khodorkovsky's plans to build a private pipeline were shelved. It is now more than a decade and a half later and there has still been no development of the Y-T field, notwithstanding the prevalence of high oil prices. In 2006, the Institute of Energy Policy in Paris, France, concluded that, "Eastern Siberia's input to the industry's development is probably overstated — this is not an oil region." The size of the prize at the Y-T field has been defined and promoted for decades by earth scientists who are research academics. As the group leader, Kontorovich holds a doctorate in Geological and Mineralogical

Sciences. This static earth science focus misses the limitations imposed by the dynamics of fluid flow, revealed through the application of reservoir simulation technology. This may change, for in 2015, Rosneft, as the new owner of East Siberia Oil and Gas Company, and China Petrochemical Corporation (Sinopec) entered into an agreement to jointly develop Y-T.

On my last evening in Moscow, Wolcott and Mach invited me to dinner, where I chose a chicken Caesar salad, declared payment beyond consulting fees for a job well done. It went down hard, as I was thinking of Wolcott's recently received performance bonus, rumored to have reached seven figures.

CHAPTER ELEVEN

SEDUCED BY GENEVA

The Managing Director of Deminex in Essen was Peter Fleimisch, the man who I had met at dinner in the home of Ivan De Grisogono. Fleimisch had jumped the sinking Deminex ship before it was sold during 1998. He had moved to Addax Petroleum in Geneva, Switzerland, taking the same title and reporting to its billionaire Swiss owner, who had previously been an oil trader. He called me during early 2001 to say that Addax needed help with reservoir simulation. The company was focused on West Africa, both onshore and offshore, with its major holdings offshore Nigeria and Cameroon. That phone call led to several short-term contracts. The first was the most important. It covered preparation of a field development plan (FDP) for the Okwori field, located 50 miles offshore Port Harcourt, Nigeria. Upon arrival at Addax, it became clear that I was replacing another consulting engineer who had been building a reservoir model for several months. He had been commuting back and forth between his home in England and Geneva on a weekly basis, and he was drained. During an overlap with him, I learned that the field is small and complex, consisting of many separate compartments, each containing either gas or oil. He had done an exemplary job using the Schlumberger modeling software, but the effort was incomplete. One of the tenets at Todd, Dietrich & Chase was that we would not use a reservoir model built by others. This was not because a model was suspected or known to be deficient — it was because of the difficulty in understanding what had already been done and the likelihood, therefore, of introducing inconsistency into the model building process. It would be like trying to finish the construction of a house without the blueprints. In this case, there was neither the time nor budget to start over, and there was no choice but to struggle.

There was a sense of ill feeling during the Okwori project and this was a forewarning of what was to come more than a year later on a return to Addax. I learned early that Fleimisch was considered to be abrasive and an outsider, not popular with the staff. He had not chosen to make a life in Geneva, instead commuting regularly on weekends to join his wife at their primary residence in the Cote d'Azur of France. That alone could not have been helpful. It was rumored that the Swiss owner had been a hands-on, energetic leader, who propelled himself around the expansive office via a foot-scooter, injecting himself into the decision making on a daily basis. Following his death in a skiing accident a month after my arrival, the staff looked to the Chief Geologist for leadership, a man who was also Swiss and retired from Royal Dutch Shell. Although highly competent, this new de facto leader was conservative and not in favor of taking on a high risk development of Okwori. He had other priorities. Fleimisch saw the potential in Okwori and wanted to move quickly to bring it on stream. Blocked internally, he chose to bring in an old friend and prior lieutenant at the now defunct Deminex, on a consulting contract to lead preparation of the necessary FDP. It soon became clear that the consultant I had replaced was weary from more than commuting — he was tired of the office politics, especially so, because he was a highly technical specialist who had little time for inefficiency. When staff input to the project was provided grudgingly, or not at all, Fleimisch gave his confidant authority to bring in several consultants, including me. Imagine the glares from staff directed at the recently arrived experts from afar in the large, open-workplace office. I was to provide the number and locations of the required wells and profiles of their expected production rates over time. My results were delivered within two months and I happily returned to California. Addax staff eventually added the critical elements of well completion design and a FPSO (floating production, storage and offloading) concept to the plan. The Nigerian Petroleum Authorities sanctioned the FDP within a year of my departure and first oil was realized in 2005.

When working on contracts for Addax, the trailing spouse (TS) and myself stayed at Hotel Adriatica, located a short distance from the office along a path running through Parc Alfred Bertrand. It's a comfortable place near the old town where many pleasant restaurants with outdoor seating are found, its one drawback being the close proximity of a hospital. Surprisingly, it was something other than helicopter and ambulance noise that was occasionally disturbing. Medical services in Switzerland, and in Thailand as we would learn later, are in demand by Gulf Arabs. I had a hunch late one night at the Adriatica as to the source of strong herb smells of saffron, garlic and curry powder, confirmed the next morning when a Swiss hotel guest confronted the head of an Arab family in the breakfast dining room, indignant about their cooking on his floor in the hotel hallways. It was amusing to witness members of very dissimilar cultures shouting and gesticulating at each other over this incident. Offsetting the negative work situation was, of course, the location of Geneva. On more than one weekend we took the train to Montreux, on the other end of Lac Leman from Geneva, there to either lunch along the lake or stay the night in Hotel Victoria Glion, positioned a thousand feet above the water with a gourmet restaurant and incredible views of the lake and Alps beyond.

It was an upcoming Easter weekend when Addax requested that I rebook my return flight to remain in Geneva for business the following week. Unable to join my TS and family in California, I treated myself to an Easter weekend at Hotel Victoria. It was expensive then and more so now — it has become a member of the elite Relais & Chateaux group. Overall, it was surprisingly a profitable weekend, as the hotel costs were partly covered by the per-diem under my contract and I was running and processing reservoir simulations on my laptop computer in the hotel room, all chargeable to the project. I ordered an unbelievable bottle of wine, drank half of it the first night and half the second, awakening Easter morning to view a beautiful carpet of snow on the ground and not lonely. What a pleasant memory! On a later weekend, a short train trip took us to Annecy, in the Rhone Alps region of southeast France, enclosing a medieval town center built around a 14th century chateau and offering a big outdoor market. We stayed in an elegant, converted Benedictine monastery next to the lake called Abbaye de Talloires, where we took in the active dinner scene as the only guests not French, witnessing the brief exchange of eye contact and head-nod that is common in Europe among persons unknown to one another, as they enter or exit a room or elevator. This simple form of social etiquette is congenial and normally not found in other areas of the world. In contrast, I recall the Sommelier showed annoyance when he saw that I had poured the bottoms of the red wine in his absence, without filtering it. He lightened up when the TS began speaking much better than expected French with him.

Working for Addax in the beautiful city of Geneva during the 4th quarter of 2002 was the most difficult time of my career. A year after leaving the Okwori project, I was offered the position of Chief Reservoir Engineer in Addax, working as a senior member of staff in Geneva. It was a flattering offer which came with a good compensation package, one which we did not turn down. Not only had I dismissed unpleasant memories of working in a big company, but I also ignored the warning signs that were fresh and still flashing, *Beware of the office politics within Addax*. In hindsight, it was the location of Geneva and its proximity to all of Europe that seduced us. At least I had made my acceptance conditional: I would report only to the Managing

Director and either side could terminate the contract without penalty anytime within the first 3 months. A day before my flight to Geneva, I was instructed to change my itinerary to stop in London, where I would meet with other Addax personnel for several days, evaluating technical data of an oil field that was a prospect for acquisition. That was all good. The problem was that the curt instruction came from someone at Addax with the title of Engineering Manager, without an introductory comment or even a hint of welcome to the company. It was before the days of text messaging or electronic mail sent via mobile phone, when a pithy message under such circumstances might be excused. The alarm bells rang and, sure enough, upon my arrival in Geneva the office politics were exploding. I was placed in the middle of it all. A search had been underway for a replacement of the Chief Reservoir Engineer, a Dutchman who had been given a notice of termination, when Fleimisch decided he wanted to short-circuit the process, taking away the plan for the Chief Geologist to interview and select the new hire.

The Chief Reservoir Engineer was still on site when I arrived, refusing to give up either his title or his desk. By Swiss labor law, and given his tenure, he had 60 days before he could be removed from his position. There was no time to push back on the chain of command that had me reporting to an Engineering Manager. That issue had to be addressed later. My first urgent task was to review and endorse a production forecast prepared by the serving Chief Reservoir Engineer, a forecast that was needed to size and order long-lead surface facilities costing nearly 100 million dollars. I was trapped! There was a major problem — the predicted ratio of gas production to oil production was much too low. I was unable to patiently ease into the new working environment by supporting what had been done by the old guard. The major reservoirs owned and operated by Addax were 3-phase systems with oil sandwiched between an overlying gas cap and an underlying aquifer, similar to those found at Zeit Bay and Yurubcheno-Tokhomskoye, but with thinner oil columns. Horizontal wells drilled into the oil bands were being produced at high rates which was an action leading to early gas breakthrough. Once the gas had reached the wells, it quickly became the dominant production phase, owing to its much higher mobility than oil or water. There was no option other than to produce the wells at higher than the critical levels to exceed the economic limit. If the wells were choked-back, they would not produce oil at economic rates. A couple of simple analytical calculations showed what was likely to be happening and the production data confirmed it: more and more gas was coming with the oil. It was only a matter of time before the oil wells morphed into gas wells, requiring very different surface facilities than those specified in the already prepared purchase orders.

There was a second problem, also of a reservoir engineering nature. Modern horizontal well technology had its inception in North America, starting with pilot wells drilled by Esso Resources Canada in its Cold Lake field in 1978. On the basis of that field test and physical model studies that preceded it, analytical equations had been developed that showed the importance of drilling horizontal wells parallel to each other. Major projects had been installed in Canada where hundreds of wells had been aligned in this manner. All of this had been presented at various technical conferences and published in the petroleum literature, yet here it was more than two decades later and there was no understanding of these findings within Addax. Well orientations were being defined by the Chief Geologist and his group, leading to a random well layout that looked like a pile of pick-up sticks, as in the popular game, rather than an array of long horizontal wells drilled parallel to each other. Wells aligned randomly are likely to accelerate the time of gas or water breakthrough and ultimately recover less oil than their parallel counterparts. It seemed no one understood or cared. The performance would look good in the short term. Just drill them and get on with it seemed to be the philosophy. How this can happen is taken up later in the Epilogue of this book.

All was lost before I arrived in Geneva. When I was unable to support the forecast prepared before my arrival, it really got ugly. I recall being told by one of the geologists, "We had a really nice little group here before you arrived." At that point, there was no downside in making an issue of my reporting channel, which was not as agreed per the contract. I asked for a meeting with the Managing Director and marched to his office with the Engineering Manager alongside. It was less than two weeks later when the TS was in California that I resigned my position, knowing there was no way forward. The avalanche that had tragically killed the owner of Addax marked the beginning of a power shift from the Managing Director to the Chief Geologist. It happened gradually, playing out during the short period of my employment. Fleimisch needed an outsider as an ally, and he was unforgiving that I would not fight the battle with him. He was gone the next year, presumably retiring from the industry along with Ivan, his good friend and my strong supporter of many years. When many of its oil wells became gas wells over time, Addax found a buyer of its declining assets in 2009. As with the East Siberian Oil and Gas Company, it seems the China Petrochemical Corporation (Sinopec) bought another company few others wanted.

Part Two

Geologists Take Over

CHAPTER TWELVE

NO COCKTAIL PARTY

We returned to our Adobe sanctuary in the Santa Ynez Valley of California from Mumbai. Shortly after our homecoming, a request was received from Addax for additional work on the Okwori field. That was followed by two consulting projects involving the injection of steam to recover heavy oil from different reservoirs in Egypt: one in the Sinai and one near the Suez Canal. None of these projects required travel away from home and that was a good thing. One of the clients with Egyptian interests was Jerry Jones, the owner of the NFL's Dallas Cowboys. During the initial telephone conversation with his agent, I recall there was no response when I jokingly said a good report would be delivered to avoid visitation from one or more of the team linebackers. The thermal reservoir simulator developed by Todd, Dietrich & Chase was used under a license agreement and the modeling was performed on my Silicon Graphics computer workstation. The project results were well received without requests for modification and there was no need to "play ball" with the client.

Then all business activity stopped for several months, prompting me to contact prior clients in search of a new project. Don Wolcott of Yukos responded quickly from Moscow, saying my timing was perfect, for Joe Mach had just fired a

British subsurface team leader. I was told there was an open position with my name on it. A written offer was shortly in-hand that stated half of the annual salary would be wired to our bank upon my acceptance. Although previously unheard of, I knew that would happen. Mach was a Senior Vice President who reported only to the CEO of the company, Mikhail Khodorkovsky. The power ceded to Mach was absolute. It was wide and deep in all matters, including those relating to the hiring, firing and treatment of both Russian and expat personnel. There was no HR Department. He was brutal in his treatment of people. Not only could he make grown men cry, he did — and he seemed to love it. How different from the Deminex workplace in Essen, where the employees were protected by the European Works Council, or the Addax workplace in Geneva where the employees were not only protected from abuse by the Swiss labor laws, they were actually capable of effectively stopping work and removing an unpopular Managing Director.

Joe Mach and Don Wolcott ran everything, from controlling the field operations in the Siberian oil fields to designing a company petroleum engineering training program in Moscow. It was ironic that two Americans had been given this much power. They hired technical experts from America, Canada, Scotland, France and the United Kingdom, many of whom were prior colleagues of Wolcott at Arco Research in Texas, who became unemployed when Arco merged with BP America, or of Mach at Schlumberger. Their dynasty became known as the Don and Joe Show.

Upon our arrival in Moscow in March, 2003, we once again chose the Savoy Hotel near the Bolshoi Theater and Red Square for our home, but this time only temporarily, while we searched for an apartment to rent. We settled on a flat in what is known as The House of Tears, a huge apartment block just across the Moscow River from the Kremlin. Built in the early 1930's, the complex was a symbol of the Great Terror of 1937 and 1938, when Stalin had hundreds of political, intellectual, economic and military elites who lived there arrested and either killed or sent to Gulags. We chose a flat on the 8th floor with a great view of the river and the Kremlin, with Saint Basil's Cathedral and Red Square in the background. It was unfurnished, with quintessential Russian parquet wood floors throughout. When inspecting the space before the arrival of the TS, a knock on the door was a surprise. Standing there was Vladimir, the building manager and a bull of a man. He had walked up 7 flights of stairs with a huge armchair on his back, offered for my use until the place was furnished. He was very proud to display his great strength, especially to an American. The empty space was an uncomfortable and creepy place to sleep before the TS arrived a few days later to furnish it.

The Yukos office was 2-½ miles from the flat, reached by walking along the Moscow River. It was a pleasant walk, with very few traffic intersections. It was good to avoid use of the underground metro system. We were on our own in Moscow, as I knew we would be, given the Yukos model and our prior contract completed two years earlier. Not surprisingly, there was no welcoming phone call or message upon our arrival. We were expected to simply find the office and show up for work on the established date.

I reported to Wolcott who had been recently promoted to Senior VP. There were two elements of my job description: first I was to provide an initial assessment of all field development plans (FDPs) prepared for Yukos oil fields, and secondly I was to mentor several young trainees in the Yukos petroleum engineering training program. Regarding the first charge, imagine how difficult it was to critique the work of several Russian project team members who had travelled to Moscow, often over great distances for periods of days on a train or in an automobile, speaking through a language translator as a foreigner, sourced in fact from a country that was a recent cold war antagonist. It was really uncomfortable when the proposed FDP was inadequate, for in that case there was no possibility of advancing the plan upward for further consideration. In essence, a negative critique meant that those coming to Moscow had to return whence they came. It was the second element of my job description that was more interesting and less stressful, at least initially. None of the trainees were employed by Yukos; first they had to successfully complete the training course. All 50 of them were university graduates, but many held degrees in areas other than science or engineering. While developing a work plan for one of the trainees assigned to me, I became interested in something called the dimensionless productivity index, abbreviated J_D. A higher J_D means more production. Mach was already a force behind using hydraulic fracturing technology to increase production in Yukos. He had invited a globally recognized expert in this technology (the late Michael Economides) to work with him (and Wolcott) in his top floor office, where they sequestered themselves for a period of weeks. Economides claimed that the maximum achievable J_D is $6/\pi$, a value that he had recently published in a popular textbook with a co-professor at the University of Houston. When pressed by Mach and others, neither the expert nor anyone else could explain why $6/\pi$ should be a limitation. I began to focus on the J_D question and became fixated on it, recalling that a little known PhD Dissertation by a Dutch colleague of mine at Shell Development Company, Jacque Hagoort, might provide the needed insight.

I started by numerically reproducing the analytical results provided by Hagoort using a reservoir simulator and then extended them, showing the derivation of $6/\pi$. It was demonstrated that this value is a theoretical maximum that applies to fractured wells that are draining a square area where the reservoir pressure is gradually depleting over time. However, in Russia, nearly all wells are being produced in response to water injection, a process designed to maintain reservoir pressure at an unchanging level. In this case, the maximum theoretical value of J_D is $4/\pi$. This work showed that Yukos was expecting better productivity improvement from hydraulic fracturing than the service companies were able to deliver. Often times there was no technical basis for the Yukos claim that a service company had done a poor job in placing a hydraulic fracture in a well, thereby opening itself up to a call for reduction of invoiced charges. Recall that Mach had moved through the revolving door from Schlumberger to his position at Yukos. He was in a powerful position. He could tell those in Schlumberger where his career had presumably stagnated that he was giving business to Halliburton, or other service companies, unless they met his demands. In fact, shortly before my arrival, he had replaced licensing agreements with Schlumberger that allowed use of the industry's standard suite of reservoir simulators with those offered by Halliburton. My J_D results weakened his ability to claim compensation for alleged poor hydraulic fracturing performance.

In closed meetings with a dozen, or more, key technical staff, the Don and Joe Show refused to accept my results, asking me instead to continue my "research" on J_D. They wanted more proof. In hindsight, what else could they do? They had fully supported the higher value of $6/\pi$ rather than $4/\pi$ and they were unwilling to alter their position. In fact, they had just prepared and submitted two manuscripts for presentation at various worldwide conferences scheduled by the Society of Petroleum Engineers, wherein $6/\pi$ was at the heart of their thesis. A few of the key technical staff understood the issue, but they remained silent. Their jobs could vanish in a flash, given an unpredictable loss of temper by Mach. Privately, they would cheer me on, vicariously fighting against the brutal arrogance of the Don and Joe Show. The interesting technical work became stressful, especially on the few occasions when Wolcott would unexpectedly visit the open office environment of the 3rd floor, there to find a group of trainees huddled around my desk, all of us animatedly discussing J_D. He needed to be viewed as the key technical man in Yukos, at all times and by all those from Mach downward to the trainees.

When math that was uncomplicated for a mathematician and challenging for me finally proved the point, I felt trapped and uncertain of my future at Yukos. And then all of the drama that had been unfolding over a period of months was suddenly trumped by a truly cataclysmic event — Mikhail Khodorkovsky was arrested by Putin. It was October 25, 2003, when he was taken at gunpoint from his corporate aircraft, after it was surrounded by police vehicles as it was readying to take off from a runway in Siberia. At the same time, Putin's agents broke into the Yukos offices, using axes to open locked filing cabinets and desks in efforts to grab possibly incriminating documents. My desk was spared damage, perhaps because it was in an open area and backed by a chalk board displaying a bunch of equations with J_D in them.

Charged with tax evasion, fraud and embezzlement, Khodorkovsky was imprisoned and not released for more than 10 years. Now residing in Switzerland at age 57 with, some say, a net worth of 250 to 500 million dollars, he heads Open Russia, a political action group that calls for democratic reforms within his mother country. His claims that the charges under which he was incarcerated were fabricated to punish him for funding political opposition to Putin were recently substantiated by an arbitration court in the Hague. It was determined that Russia must pay 50 billion dollars to the shareholders and former employees of Yukos, a private company which was forced into bankruptcy by ever increasing claims for back-taxes, before its assets were sold in a rigged auction to the state-owned Rosneft and Gazprom energy giants. The main production unit of Yukos was sold for 9.4 billion dollars to a front company registered in a grocery store in a regional town, which was then bought by Rosneft. The same asset was later valued at 60 billion dollars when its shares were floated on the London Stock Exchange. The figures kept changing in Putin's favor, but the rules of the game did not — the tax bills always had to exceed the total value of the Yukos assets and they did. Funding political opposition was only one of several reasons for Khodorkovsky's arrest. Putin wanted authoritarian rule and that was not possible without state control of the oil industry. The planned sale of selected Yukos assets to ExxonMobil and opening discussions with the Chinese regarding construction of a private pipeline to move oil from Yukos oil fields in Eastern Siberia to China may have been two other reasons for his seizure.

Just as the U.S. Government will unlikely compensate Chevron shareholders in its sale of the Elk Hills Naval Petroleum Reserve, the Russian Government will unlikely compensate Yukos shareholders for its expropriation of that company. In the one case, Al Gore Senior and Al Gore Junior both benefited from political favors and employment compensation after their public service. In the other, Putin has reportedly siphoned off vast sums of public funds sourced from the breakup of Yukos to build his palace on the Black Sea. Shareholders began seizing Russian bank deposits in Paris and other French cities during 2015, and a French court has rejected recent Russian requests to suspend these seizures.

Prior to Khodorkovsky's arrest, the Don and Joe Show had instructed all of the senior expat staff to remain in Moscow for a Christmas and New Year's cocktail party to be given by Khodorkovsky. The TS and I were really looking forward to the event and had not made plans to return to California for the holidays. That disappointment was eclipsed by other news that was about to break: I would soon be unemployed. Mach summoned me and 2 other senior technical people — all of us expats — to his office about 6 weeks after our CEO had been taken down. He purportedly wanted an understanding of J_D. In hindsight, it seems he had been told it was time to start paring the expat staff and he was simply starting with me. His approach was masterful. By repeatedly interrupting the discussion of J_D, saying, "You would make more of a contribution working for our cross-town competitor, TNK-BP," he was cleverly attacking my ego. It was all a ploy to get a declaration of, "I quit," before he had to use the substitute, "You're fired." Use of the latter phrase would ostensibly leave open the possibility of legal action taken for an early termination. The two other expats were present unknowingly to confirm which phrase was voiced, if necessary. In fact, neither phrase was voiced. I left Mach hearing an expletive and called the TS from a pub. The next day, I learned that a bonus had been wired to our bank, and it was surprisingly on deposit prior to receiving the summons to meet with Mach. Preparing for our exodus, we gave our friends keys to the flat and invitations to help themselves to any of the remaining furniture. It was later learned that Vladimir had beaten them all to the spoils. We returned to California at the beginning of 2004. Later I would learn that all of the expat talent was gone from Yukos within 4 months of my departure.

The group that had been surreptitiously working for weeks in Mach's penthouse office, taking in results being passed upward to them from my 3rd floor desk, later authored and presented two technical papers to the Society of Petroleum Engineers after my departure, presenting my results on J_D as if they were their own. They presented $4/\pi$ and all that it meant as if there had never been a question of its application, but only after my departure. It was surprising that my work had not been referenced by any of these authors.

The Don and Joe Show continue to slip and slide around in the oil industry. They resurfaced after the demise of Yukos in a publically traded company on the London Stock Exchange, called RusPetro Plc, where Wolcott served as the CEO and Mach served as a non-executive board member. They both moved on in 2013, owing reportedly to poor performance and a severe overstatement of reserves in the single company asset, a Russian oil field. A year later, they reappeared as non-executive board members of Petroceltic International, Plc., a company headquartered in Dublin, where they quickly resigned upon losing a vote by shareholders to unseat the incumbent CEO. The Don and Joe Show were reportedly sponsored in this effort by Worldview Capital Management SA, a hedge fund representing Bulgarian and Russian investors. A motivation for the takeover attempt was purportedly an opportunity to reduce income tax paid by the investors. Who knows what the next escapade will be for these two characters? It was a fascinating time with Yukos for the 9-month duration of the contract. The only real regret was missing the cocktail party, where we would have been personally introduced to Mikhail Khodorkovsky, one of our very few heroes in the oil business.

Loss of the Yukos job really jolted us. Upon our return to the United States we were homeless. We had sold the Adobe, expecting to be living in Russia for years. Two months later we had purchased a home in the desert of California, unsure of whether we again would have an overseas adventure. How could we know there would be one after another of them over the next 10 years?

Schlumberger called as we were settling into our new home to offer another project in Moscow, this time for a company called SeverTEK, a joint venture owned equally by the Finnish energy company Fortum and the Russian oil company Lukoil. The joint venture had recently acquired the rights to develop 5 small oil fields, the largest of which was called South Shapkino, located about 1200 miles north of Moscow beneath a reindeer farm. There was no need to visit the field, as my technical focus was on all things underground, not on the surface. I traveled to Moscow ahead of the TS in the normal manner and checked into the Budapest Hotel, more affordable than the Savoy and centrally located near the SeverTEK office and the Bolshoi Theater. SeverTEK had hired a project manager by the name of Tom Godfrey, an American who had moved through the Schlumberger revolving door to work for them, just as Don Wolcott and Joe Mach had moved through that same door to work for Yukos. Godfrey had been educated as a nuclear engineer at the University of Colorado in Boulder, known to be a good academic institution and a first-tier party school. Godfrey was unmarried and fluent in the Russian language. He had been partying hard and working in Russia for many years. As a result, he was well connected with expatriates and natives alike, both young and old. He seemed to be of the same breed as Wolcott, easily leaving a life in America to seek his fortune in a foreign land, with little or no intention of returning.

It's a lot less difficult to build a fortune where income is either not taxed, or taxed at a much lower rate than in one's home country. An American is one of the few, if only, nationals who is required to pay tax on income earned from foreign sources. It was irksome to personally work with British, Canadian, Danish, Dutch, French, German, Indian, and Italian consultants, knowing that their after tax income was 30% higher, or more, than mine, particularly when my taxes were being used to disproportionately support NATO, the IMF, the UN and other institutions benefitting them. The injustice and big sums of money involved provide a strong motivation for an American not to declare income earned abroad to the Internal Revenue Service and State Franchise Tax Boards! Once an American expat starts on a path of tax avoidance, the price he must pay in back-taxes for returning to live in the United States is often so high that it effectively prevents him from returning home. American self employed contractors and consultants are most at risk in this matter, for when they choose, they can simply stop filing income tax returns once out of the country. It's their decision and theirs alone. The TS and I met more than a few American couples who had chosen self-imposed exile. In an effort to improve tax compliance, Vladimir Putin had reduced the personal income tax rate to 13% in the Russian Federation, effective January 1, 2001. And as an incentive to attract talent to the deserts of the United Arab Emirates, the income tax rate there was zero. While working and socializing with other Americans in those countries, it was not rare to hear them say after a few cocktails, "Panama (or Chile, or Sardinia) is a marvelous place and we are looking forward to retiring there." The elephant at the bar was the topic of tax avoidance and it was never raised.

The return to Moscow allowed me to personally meet there with the accounting firm of Ernst & Young, who were advising prior Yukos employees on how to calculate and pay income tax owed to the Russian Federation for the prior year (2003). Yukos were covering the cost of this service per my earlier contract with them. It was learned that Yukos had reported only 2.5%

of the salary I had received and tax withholding in compliance with a tax rate of 30% applying to consultants working short-term in Russia. Yukos had not reported 97.5% of my total salary that had been paid through a bank in Cyprus — and, supposedly, they were legally not required to do so. Ernst & Young stated, "Other Yukos people have declared the Cyprus paid salary, 'It is up to you to do so, or not' and, 'Given a decision not to declare this income, if ever audited, you will be in trouble.'" Upon my return to California, I wire-transferred tens of thousands of dollars to a bank in Moscow for further transmittal to the Russian tax authorities, per instructions from Ernst & Young. Prior to doing so, I first reviewed the entire matter with an American colleague working for Ernst & Young in their Moscow office, who confirmed the owed amount and the legal ability to substantially reduce our tax obligation in the United States using taxes already paid in Russia. The TS and I wanted to feel unthreatened while standing in the Immigration line upon reentering Russia in the future. We did not want to think about the elephant at the bar when out to dinner with other American expats. And, more importantly, we wanted to keep open the option of living and retiring in the United States without the peril of owed back-taxes.

South Shapkino was producing nearly 30,000 barrels of oil per day (BDO) and the operator wanted to raise that level to 50,000 BDO, by drilling additional wells and installing a pattern waterflood. Reporting to Godfrey, my job was to build a reservoir model and to calibrate it by reproducing historical production rates and pressures. Once calibrated, the model would provide a good estimate for how much oil was in the reservoir. It was to be used after my departure by others as a predictor of future reservoir performance.

The SeverTEK office was headed by a senior employee from Fortum, who called me to a private meeting late one evening. It was just the two of us without the presence of a co-owning Lukoil representative. It was reiterated that SeverTEK had hired Schlumberger as its major consulting firm and Godfrey as the project manager. Godfrey, in turn, with the support of Lukoil had hired a Russian consultancy, Enconco, to provide a second opinion on the volume of oil-in-place and remaining oil reserves. Fortum called the meeting to let me know they were soon planning to sell their half interest and would benefit from a high estimate of future oil recovery. They were concerned that the Russians (Godfrey, Enconco and Lukoil) were working to skew the numbers toward a low estimate of remaining oil reserves, as the probable future buyer of Fortum's half interest. It was a project with long days of intense work and a duration of two months, made all the more difficult by a lack of trust between the joint venture owners. Unlike the U.S. Department of Energy in the Elk Hills project, SeverTEK quickly paid my final invoices, presumably because they felt the numbers were fairly developed without bias.

CHAPTER THIRTEEN

THE WATCH
AND NECKTIE

It was good to be home in the desert of California, even in the summer when the temperature occasionally reached 115°F. During this downtime, I had a chance to reflect on how the petroleum consulting business was changing. The year was 2004. Prior to that date, virtually all of my contracts were sourced from colleagues and people known to me. I had always been retained as a consultant, working in an independent manner and deciding the technical approach taken to satisfy a defined scope of work. I normally sat down with a prospective client to learn what he needed in a pre-proposal meeting, before writing a proposal that covered what was to be delivered, over what period of time and for how much money. The control was mine alone and I was free to hire associates with special skill sets when necessary. I was without a boss, following a business style that I first knew was for me as a student in 1964, when I was introduced to owners of a consulting civil engineering firm in Santa Barbara, California. They were independent and free to decide their business interests!

Starting about the time of the new millennium, oil companies began using staffing agencies to find earth scientists and petroleum engineers willing to work in their offices on a contract basis. The term *consultant* had gradually been replaced by the term *contractor*. Working as an adjunct to staff, a contractor performs under the direction of a company employee. After nearly 40 years in the industry, most of my colleagues were either retired, or worse. We were no longer able to refer each other for opportunities. I thought my network was gone. If I wanted to remain active in business, it was necessary to change with the times, by posting my resume on the Internet. It was July when a call came in from Oilfield Production Consultants (OPC), a consultancy located in London that seconds contract staff into clients' offices. They had found me by searching for key words present in my resume. I agreed with their request to put me forward for a contract position with ExxonMobil in Hanover, Germany. It must have been the combination of a strong resume and my German surname that sealed the deal, for I was unknown there. The TS and I were on German soil 6 weeks later, following the receipt of a work permit from the German authorities and a signed contract with OPC.

By using a third party agent, a company wanting to retain an adjunct to staff could remain at arms length with all matters pertaining to the contract. As at Yukos, there was no welcoming message of any type upon our arrival in Hanover. We were on our own, in the manner we preferred, however in this case we were unable to find an accommodation. All hotels had been booked a year, or more, in advance by business people participating in an industrial trade fair, known in Germany as a *messe*, which basically takes over a city like Hanover, Berlin or Munich for a week or two, commonly during the month of April, the month of our arrival. We rented a car and found a hotel in Celle, located about 25 miles northeast of Hanover, where we set up residence for a few weeks until we found a flat to rent in Hanover for the duration of the project. The only space available was found by the TS. It was the middle floor of a 3-story private home, located in a residential neighborhood and reached by a 15 minute walk from the ExxonMobil office. The landlord and his wife occupied the ground floor and their daughter and son-in-law occupied the top floor with their two children. This was an arrangement to be avoided, except that each floor was completely separated from another and each had its own entrance.

The giant Soehlingen gas field in Germany was discovered in 1980. It is owned by BEB (a 50/50 German gas joint venture between ExxonMobil and Royal Dutch/Shell), RWE-DEA and Wintershall AG. There are three reservoirs within the field, called the Havel, Wustrow and Dethlingen. The first two are much more permeable than the third, meaning that fluids flow at higher rates through them in response to an applied pressure differential than through the tighter rock of the Dethlingen. The better quality Havel and Wustrow reservoirs were the first to be developed and they were nearly depleted. Massive amounts of gas remain in the Dethlingen where the tight rock must be hydraulically fractured to unlock its potential. It was Mobil in 1978 who first showed the potential of giant diatomite reservoirs in California by hydraulically fracturing a well in the South Belridge field, establishing value recognized by Shell when they bought the interests of Belridge Oil Company a year later for 3.65 billion dollars, then the largest merger of two companies in the United States. In 1993, the German affiliate of Mobil drilled a horizontal well in the Soehlingen field to demonstrate that two existing technologies (hydraulic fracturing and horizontal drilling) could be combined to unlock the huge gas reserves of the Dethlingen reservoir. By using a technique called stage fracturing, 4 hydraulically induced fractures were sequentially placed along the 2,000-foot horizontal section of the demonstration well to allow gas to flow at commercial rates from the low permeability reservoir. This same combination of two technologies had been pioneered by Maersk Oil in the Danish sector of the North Sea, six years earlier. The shale fracturing revolution in the United States started 10 years after the Soehlingen pilot demonstration project when the technology had advanced to allow the use of much longer horizontal wells containing many more hydraulically-induced fractures.

My job was to review models built for the Havel and Wustrow reservoirs by ExxonMobil staff that had been incapable of reproducing the long history of field performance during reservoir simulation. I was to critique them and explain why they had not been useful. The project was to run for 6 months. A longer duration was not possible due to immigration and taxation rules applying to contractors who were not citizens of a country belonging to the European Union. I could not work longer than 6 months in Germany, nor could I work longer than 10.75 hours in any one day. This project was to mark the first time I would be working as a contractor, rather than as a consultant. I would be working under the direction of a company employee and I was uneasy about that. I definitely wanted the control. I had learned over 35 years that it was essential to name and empower a principal model architect. One person needs absolute control of how all the pieces fit together. He needs to start with the end in-mind, with an understanding of how the static description of a reservoir affects the fluid dynamics during the modeling process. The principal model architect needs an understanding of both geology and reservoir engineering.

As expected, on my first day as a contractor I was introduced to a staff geologist who was to be the project manager. He had about 20 years with ExxonMobil and he was adept at running the powerful reservoir modeling software developed by Schlumberger. During the first minutes of our conversation, the alarm bells began to silently ring. I had read a publication on the subject reservoirs that told me the pore space in the rocks had been partially filled with clay over geologic time, in a process called diagenesis. For all practical purposes, the distribution of porosity and permeability in diagenetically altered porous media is spatially unpredictable, and this calls for a random distribution of rock properties while building the models. The powerful Schlumberger Petrel™ software is one package that can be used for this purpose, but the procedures are seemingly not taught in training classes or described in training manuals. As later confirmed, it was the determinism introduced during the property modeling step that rendered the ExxonMobil models incapable of reproducing the performance history of the reservoirs. It would be a tall order to change the views of the project manager in this key technical area, especially while working as a contract reservoir engineer.

Fortunately, conflict was avoided. All the anxiety faded away when I learned the entire ExxonMobil work group were needed to prepare for a major audit called by Shell. The subsurface manager apologized and asked if I might work solo during the 6 months in Hannover. Working as a consultant after all, I reported to a German reservoir engineer (Gerald Stanke), who more than anyone, before or since, understood the random property modeling work flows of my approach, developed 10 years earlier while consulting for Deminex. In his own style and language, he explained it to his colleagues and it was enthusiastically accepted, apparently by all. The project went well. On my last day I was presented with an ExxonMobil wristwatch and necktie! I had narrowly dodged the situation of having to work under the direction of another person. There would be no further escapes. In every future contract, I would be reporting to a company geologist as an adjunct to staff in what ultimately became a series of failed ventures, failure in the sense that the modeling was not capable of reproducing the historical reservoir performance.

CHAPTER FOURTEEN

COPENHAGEN HYGGE

During the last month with ExxonMobil, the TS and I flew to Copenhagen for a long weekend. While walking along the North Sea to view the Little Mermaid, we passed the impressive offices of The Maersk Group, a global business conglomerate with container shipping and energy its core activities. Maersk had owned an interest in the Dow-Chanslor lease of the Belridge oil field in California, operated by the Crutcher-Tufts Corporation, the first client of The Dietrich Corporation. Maersk had placed one of their young petroleum engineers in the Crutcher-Tufts office to look after their interests. Steen Koefed is his name and I got to know him while providing consulting services over a period of several years. Steen bought a little sports car and loved driving it around Bakersfield, while wearing a Danish cap and soaking up the Southern California sun. It seemed he had been saddened to return to Copenhagen, where he had eventually reached the position of Senior Vice President in Maersk Oil. I shared this history with the TS while gazing at the statue of the Little Mermaid, which is only a few feet tall and true to its name. I thought it was really a long shot that we might secure a contract with Maersk in the beautiful city of Copenhagen. Telephoning Steen was a good thing to do. He was immediately keen to bring me into Maersk on a six-month contract, starting as soon as possible.

Working for Maersk and reporting to a Senior Vice President had its advantages. It was a direct hire position with a simple contract to sign and without the staffing agency middleman. I arrived in Copenhagen about a week prior to the TS, after finishing ExxonMobil and relaxing for a few weeks in the California desert. It was early May and the project would run for 6 months, during the best months of weather in Denmark. I checked into the Admiral Hotel, an old timbered grain storage building on the wharf near the Maersk office. There was a beautiful view of the new Copenhagen Opera House across the harbor and it was really pleasant to jog alongside the moored boats on the weekend.

Steen had changed during the 15 years since I had last seen him. His physical appearance had not changed much. Tall and of athletic build, he still fit the image of a Viking. He was proud that his ancestors had temporarily repelled Swedes from invading Bornholm, a Danish island in the Baltic Sea to the east of Denmark and separated from it by Sweden. His change was more of an emotional nature. He was somber, perhaps due to the long gray winter months that were just ending and the pressure that came with his job. The Danish word *hygge* translates roughly to the state of being cozy, as in basking in the warm glow of candlelight, creating a warm atmosphere, sharing picnics in the park, and enjoying the good things in life with family and friends. Hygge helps one get through the long, dark winters. Perhaps Steen had not been getting enough of it. It was no surprise there was no welcoming upon my arrival in the city, nor later at any time. I knew there was nothing personal about his remoteness. As we had learned while living in Oslo on contract with Deminex, Scandinavians rarely socialize outside of their family group. The TS found an incredible furnished apartment within a few days of her arrival. It was positioned on the top floor of a 17th century building on Gothersgade, a street forming an edge to the Rosenborg Castle Gardens, a public park housing a Dutch Renaissance palace with a museum where the crown jewels are on display. We were handed the keys to our apartment by a housing agency before signing a tenant's contract or paying any rental fees. A contract with Maersk Oil was enough to literally open doors!

Maersk is best known by its container ships and bulk carriers seen in ports all over the world, each displaying the distinctive emblem that is a 7-point white star embedded in a blue background. A. P. Moeller Maersk A/S was granted a concession to survey and exploit oil and natural gas resources in the Danish sector of the North Sea in 1962, rendering it an almost monopoly-like status. It was a 40-year agreement, calling for a levy of 69% to be paid to the state, a tax that was fixed and not related to oil price. Maersk McKinney Moeller was the son of the founder and company chairman until age 90, a time reached just prior to my arrival. His philanthropy was unmatched by any other in Denmark. He had the Copenhagen Opera House designed and donated to the state several years before the oil and gas concession was set to expire. It was reportedly the most expensive opera house ever built, and renewal of the 40-year concession under the same terms must have been one of the most lucrative ever granted. The terms remained unchanged, notwithstanding higher duties that were being paid by other North Sea operators. Norway was receiving a levy of 80% and the levy paid to the United Kingdom had recently been changed to float with the oil price. Mr. Moeller liked formality. We were required to wear a coat and necktie when away from our desks and a necktie while at our desks. I liked the discipline and structure. He still served as a major company owner and I would occasionally see him arriving and leaving the office, once brushing my desk on the way to meet the driver of his modest Audi automobile, pleased to see that I was wearing a necktie. At the time, the Maersk family owned about 53% of the company stock and reportedly controlled 70% of the voting. The flagship building where I worked housed employees of both Maersk Oil and Maersk Shipping. Although all shared the complimentary daily breakfast and lunch in a large cafeteria, the two groups seemingly did not mix and I regret not learning about the shipping business. It was rumored that the shipping business was highly competitive and that Maersk Oil was the most profitable enterprise. Indeed, oil and gas activity provided the Maersk Group with 22% of its revenue and 68% of its profit in 2008.

Three titans of industry had now crossed my path, each a multi-billionaire and among the most wealthy in the world: Paul Whittier of Belridge Oil Company, Mikhail Khodorkovsky of Yukos Oil Corporation and Maersk McKinney Moeller of Maersk Oil. All had been huge philanthropists and popular with the masses, unlike the financial moguls of Wall Street. These oilmen inherited or built privately owned and controlled empires. They alone were responsible for the financial risks of their decisions. Their actions and the reputation of the family name were linked, not unlike those of the partners at the Wall Street investment banks, for example Solomon Brothers, J.P. Morgan, or Goldman Sachs, prior to their conversion from private partnerships to public corporations. It was John Gutfreund, the former CEO of Salomon Brothers, who turned that firm into Wall Street's first public corporation in 1981, thereby setting up a business model in which the financial risk was transferred from private individuals to public shareholders and ultimately the U.S. Government. Dubbed the King of Wall Street for taking this lead, Gutfreund turned an investment bank into a gambling casino, reportedly breaking his promise never to sell the partnership and incurring the outrage of the other Wall Street firms. When describing his career at a commencement ceremony of Columbia business school following the 2008 financial crisis, it's said that he wept at the podium, imploring the new graduates to chose a profession other than Wall Street.

There was no need for us to rent a car in Copenhagen. It was a 30 minute walk to the office, reached via traversing scenic parklands at each end of the route. On my first day at work, I learned that I would not be reporting to Steen. Instead, I would be reporting to a production engineer who had been named as the manager of a new project. A production engineer is a specialist in wellbore technology and operations. He usually has no experience with building reservoir models or using them to simulate reservoir performance. The project manager had placed a young geologist in charge of building the reservoir model and a reservoir engineer in charge of simulation. It was to be a Danish led effort, with HS consigned to a position of assisting the Danish reservoir engineer. This type of low level assignment was unprecedented, yet I would encounter it for years to come. It was time to leave my ego at home if I wanted to work at all. In the absence of strong leadership from a senior manager, why would local staff cede control to an outsider? I was embedded in a team who were responsible for improving performance from the chalk reservoirs of the Valdemar field, located in the Danish sector of the North Sea. It was an open office environment where eight of us sat side by side in a common room. When it became clear that the model building was off track, it was difficult to get the ear of the project manager without all hearing of it. Steen failed to engage, remaining aloof and remote down the hall in his separate office, reachable only when his secretary allowed. Soon it was clarified that my role was to serve as a mentor to the reservoir engineer who would be running the simulator. After a few months, the reservoir model was supposedly ready and it was passed to the Dane in charge of simulation. It was necessary to demonstrate that the model was capable of simulating the 10 years of historical reservoir performance before it could be used to predict future oil recovery. This is called the history matching step in reservoir simulation. It is a crucial step that utterly failed in this case. Reservoir characterization was the problem and this was owned by the project geologist. Failure is serious when assigned staff spend months without results. It was especially painful in this case, because Maersk was acting as the field operator, spending funds allocated to the project by its partners — Chevron, Shell and a group called the Danish North Sea Fund — and answerable to them.

The Danish reservoir engineer became the goat. He voluntarily left the company to join Danish Oil and Natural Gas (DONG) in Copenhagen. I was covered from damage. In what would become standard practice for all my future projects, I wrote a series of memos describing what needed to be done to develop a suitable model, distributing them to team members and managers alike, without critiquing the work of others. Colleagues present at my going-away luncheon were too young to remember the theme song of Bob Hope, "Thanks for the Memories," and they were unaware that I borrowed those words, emphasizing *Memories* to get a laugh during a farewell toast. It's puzzling why Steen did not support me in a leadership position. Perhaps he tried and was blocked by less senior staff who were not willing to accept a specialist from afar, brought in by their Senior Vice President. Recall that this very same story occurred at Addax Petroleum in Geneva where mutinous behavior was believed to be rooted in the Swiss labor laws. There, the Managing Director had been effectively forced out by the company staff. Whether in response to staff sentiment or calls from the Board of Directors, Steen left the company a few years later. He reportedly became Head of Global Development for Wintershall in Rijswijk, Netherlands.

Reservoir simulation was not the strong suit of Maersk. They were expert in offshore drilling and operations, not unpredictable given their Viking heritage. Their chalk reservoirs are of low permeability, like the diatomite reservoirs of California and the siltstone reservoirs of the Soehlingen field in Germany. Their wells are of low productivity and expensive to place in the offshore environment. Analytical calculations showed that productivity could be greatly improved by drilling a horizontal well and hydraulically fracturing it, leading Maersk to successfully pilot test this combination of two existing technologies in the Dan field in 1987. That pioneering demonstration led to further development of the Dan field and the common use of multiply-fractured horizontal wells throughout the industry. That same year, Phillips Petroleum was more concerned about just being able to continue production from their chalk reservoirs, never mind their productivity. In their Ekofisk field offshore Norway, the air gaps (the minimum clearance between mean water level and the top sides structure of an offshore platform) were shrinking alarmingly. Several of their fixed-leg platforms were gradually sinking below the waves as the ocean floor was subsiding. Fluid production from the diatomite reservoirs in California causes surface subsidence — production from chalk reservoirs does the same. Diatomite and chalk are similar. They are known as cohesive rocks and both are highly compressible. The big difference is there's nothing above the diatomite reservoirs except the sage brush of the San Joaquin Valley, whereas billions of dollars of offshore infrastructure overlies the chalk reservoirs of the North Sea. Water injection had effectively stopped subsidence in the light oil diatomite reservoirs where steam injection was not required to recover deposits of heavy (or viscous) oil. When the air gaps started to shrink, Phillips Petroleum began injecting water, surprisingly with little effect. Later it was realized that chalk is unusual because its solubility in water increases, rather than decreases, with decreasing temperature. Years of injecting cold North Sea water as a means of hopefully controlling ocean floor subsidence had just dissolved the chalk and made the situation worse! In a similar manner, the industry had learned that injecting steam to recover heavy oil from diatomite increases the density of the rock through geochemical processes, thereby setting up stresses that lead to uncontrollable surface subsidence. Reservoir simulators are now capable of predicting stress and temperature-induced subsidence using laboratory measurements on rock samples. Phillips Petroleum spent an estimated 1.25 billion of today's dollars and employed 15,000 people to jack-up the offshore platforms by 6 meters, allowing them to continue producing the Ekofisk oil reserves for a number of additional years.

Maersk was on the lookout for the effects of reservoir compaction and ocean floor subsidence caused by their operations at Valdemar. They purposely choked back their production wells to limit the damage and avoided water injection. When the reservoir model built by the project geologist was shelved, there were still months to run on my contract. Rather than send me home, I was asked for a proposal on how to use reservoir simulation to optimize the development of Valdemar using multiply-fractured horizontal wells. While on contract with BP in Houston during 1991, I had been given access to a Cray YM-P supercomputer, a machine costing millions of dollars and, at the time, by far the most powerful in the world. It allowed detailed evaluation of horizontal well productivity using reservoir simulation. I learned a lot about the modeling procedures necessary for accurate numerical results, by first using high-resolution reservoir models to reproduce complex analytical solutions as a way to tune, or calibrate, the reservoir simulation model. The results were published in the Canadian Journal of Petroleum Technology, there to receive the best paper award for 1996. I generally agree with the TS that a technical publication and a dime may get the author a cup of coffee, at most. However, in this case, there was a payoff. Maersk liked the proposal and allowed me to work solo, using the simulator to estimate the likely interference effects between adjacently drilled wells and between propped hydraulic fractures. The practical outcome was a recommendation on spacing: how close to space the horizontal wells drilled parallel to each other and what distance should be maintained between the hydraulically induced fractures.

During the last month of my contract, I was transferred to another group to evaluate the oil recovery potential of a well drilled on the edge of the Halfdan field. When looking at the reservoir model being used for this purpose by an employee taking a leave of absence from the company, I was unable to work with it. Once again, HS was refusing to endorse the in-progress reservoir modeling at Maersk. I was given the freedom to rebuild the reservoir model and use it to justify the drilling of an edge well at Halfdan. During my last days in Copenhagen, Steen asked me to contact Maersk six months later, when I could again legally enter Denmark on a new work permit, for the purpose of preparing a field development plan (FDP) for Halfdan. When I did so, the staff understandably said, "He's a good engineer, but too independent for us." It would be 7 years before I secured a second contract with Maersk in Denmark.

CHAPTER FIFTEEN

BANGKOK BUDDHISM

OPC called again during my last days at Maersk, asking whether I would be interested in working with Chevron in Bangkok, Thailand. I recall slipping away to an empty conference room to privately take the telephone interview from Chevron. Incredibly, one of the interviewers was known to me from the Chevron / U.S. Department of Energy (DOE) equity dispute at Elk Hills Naval Petroleum Reserve in California, the contentious project where I had been retained as the Independent Petroleum Engineer chosen by the U.S. Secretary of Energy, to play the classic role of a consultant.

The new project was unusual for Chevron and most in the industry. The issue was produced water reinjection (PWRI) in the Gulf of Thailand. Reservoir water naturally produced with the oil and separated from it on the offshore production facility contained concentrations of arsenic and mercury that exceeded safe levels for human tolerance. The produced water was being separated from the oil and simply over-boarded into the Gulf of Thailand, in a manner that was in compliance with legal requirements that were set to change. Chevron needed a project manager for PWRI, to lead the effort on finding a disposal site for the produced water, other than the Gulf of Thailand. This sounded interesting. It would be a way of helping to protect the environment. The oil-bearing formation underlying Chevron's facility is the same formation found at shallow depths beneath the country of Bangladesh, where drinking water supplied from wells has led to arsenic poisoning of tens of millions of people. Although this project would have no impact on the Bangladesh problem, it would return the naturally occurring, produced toxins to a safe underground storage site.

I flew from Copenhagen to Bangkok over a weekend, without returning home. OPC handed me over to a Dutch staffing agency (Brunel) that has offices in 40 countries, many of them in Asia and South East Asia, presumably because OPC was not registered to conduct business in Thailand. In the standard manner, one did not ask about what the staffing agencies were being paid by the clients. It was rumored that the markup of charges for professional services was near 20%. It was important to control my pay rate for professional services (net of any and all imposed foreign taxes and fees), excluding living and travel-related expenses, which were highly variable due to location. My daily rate for professional services had been USD 720 during 1985 and USD 1,280 during 2014. That was an average yearly increase of 2.7%, a number which was below the average yearly increase due to inflation of 4.1%. After adjusting for inflation, the compensation received by a reservoir engineering consultant or contractor had gradually dropped over time. Reasons for the fall probably include fees charged by the staffing agency middlemen and the increased number of skilled workers applying for the same position.

Upon arrival in Bangkok, I was met at the airport by a Brunel driver holding up a little sign with my name on it. He drove me to the Hilton Sukhumvit Bangkok, located in the heart of all the action. It was hot and humid, no place for the heavy wool clothing brought directly from Copenhagen. On my first work day, I donned a double-breasted blue blazer with its gold colored metal buttons and matching necktie, one without the ExxonMobil oil derricks on it that was the departing gift in Hanover. While walking a few blocks to my appointment with Brunel, I was waiting to cross a wide intersection where traffic was being controlled by a Thai policeman. He must have seen the reflection of sunlight off the six blazer buttons — he blew long and hard into his whistle, stopping traffic in all directions, probably thinking he was assisting a VIP, recently arrived to meet the King of Thailand.

The TS arrived a few days later, bringing my warm weather clothing and saving me from receiving more teasing comments at the office, where it was short sleeves and open collars. A foreigner, so-called specialist, need not dress like one. It was a good thing meeting George McNeal, a Canadian petroleum engineer who had been living and working in Thailand for a few years. He owned a place in Phuket and was renting in Bangkok, while consulting for the same Chevron group with which I would be working. George alerted us to the traffic patterns of Bangkok and the information was priceless. We avoided Sukhumvit where nearly all expats live, choosing instead a location on the Chao Phraya River, 25 minutes from the office. A serviced apartment was available at Lebua State Tower, looking out through a wall of windows at the meandering, snake-like river, 37 floors below. We tried it for a few nights and decided instead on an identical unit available on the 24th floor. We had heard about a mock fire drill that had taken place a few months earlier, when the stair wells had been plugged by residents who could not move quickly. I bought a self contained breathing apparatus for each of us, good for 10 minutes in the event we needed to escape to the street level. The flat was ideal, like a suite. It had a double door entry, and the service was typical Asian, impeccable. It was repeatedly necessary to ask the service staff not to change the bedding in the 2nd bedroom daily, as no one was using that room. Lebua State Tower is one of the tallest buildings in Asia. It has the distinction of housing the world's highest outdoor restaurant and bar, positioned 64 floors up with a glass wall 5 feet in height running the perimeter of the place. It's called *Sirocco*. Those not afflicted by acrophobia can inch up to the glass and peer into the abyss. The view of Bangkok is unmatched. Reached by a separate elevator, entry is controlled with a casual smart dress code, to stop access by those wearing sleeveless T-shirts and flip-flops, a description applying most often to Aussie men on vacation with a local Thai girl in tow.

Near State Tower and on the same side of the river are the Mandarin Oriental and The Shangri-La hotels. The Peninsula Bangkok is reached by a short ferry ride across the river. All are affordable luxury hotels with live music, evening buffets and weekend luncheons that are world class. A Dutch colleague who I had met while at ExxonMobil in Hanover spoke often of retiring soon in Bangkok to play golf and enjoy life. It was not before I had lived there for months that I understood the lure. Each morning and evening I would hail a taxi on the street for commuting to and from the office. It was necessary to walk a block away from the hotel and office to secure the best taxi fares. When it rained, the wait for a taxi could be interminable. Otherwise, it was a quick commute.

Chevron had just merged with Union Oil Company of California (Unocal) and were operating more than 180 offshore platforms in the Gulf of Thailand. A lean staff were scheduling and managing 5 drilling rigs simultaneously. The work was intense and made all the more difficult by the need for integrating Unocal people into the business. In 1962, Unocal had been the first company awarded exploration rights by the Kingdom of Thailand. They drilled a gas discovery well in 1972. This was their turf and they were not happy to be a new wholly owned subsidiary of Chevron. A year after the merger, it was not uncommon to be handed a business card with that ubiquitous Unocal logo on it, a bright blue "76" written on an orange ball.

Chevron also had been an early entrant in Thailand, operating there since 1962. In 1999, they acquired a 52% interest in the offshore Block B8/32, where as operator they began aggressive development of the Benchamas and Tantawan oil fields. Oil and gas reservoirs are present in thick sedimentary sequences in the Gulf of Thailand, where most of the individual reservoir units do not extend laterally over long distances. Since the pore space containing hydrocarbons is poorly connected, water injection for the purpose of maintaining reservoir pressure and improving oil recovery had generally not been used. That had changed in later years. In this type of geologic setting, it's necessary to rely on so-called classical reservoir engineering methods to predict reservoir performance, rather than on reservoir simulation. I had not been hired to design a waterflood or field development plan using a simulator. Reporting to a legacy Chevron petroleum engineer, my job was to determine where to dispose of the water that is co-produced with the oil. I was initially asked to review a technical report newly prepared by Advanced Geotechnology, Inc. (AGI), a Canadian consulting firm providing services to the PWRI project. AGI had conducted and interpreted a mini-frac test in a water-filled, sandstone formation overlying the oil bearing reservoirs at Benchamas, as a means of evaluating the potential for storing the produced water in a natural aquifer. The concept was to hydraulically fracture the aquifer in a water disposal well to achieve good injectivity of the produced water. Once again, it was necessary for HS to question and not support what was in progress, all shortly after his arrival. Unlike diatomite or chalk, sandstone has a low compressibility that is not much different from the compressibility of water. It was likely that good injectivity could initially be obtained, but there was little storage capacity in the aquifer. The reservoir pressure would rapidly rise to dangerous levels after storing only a fraction of the required water disposal volumes. AGI had applied its proprietary software that was formulated to predict single well performance, not reservoir performance. The focus of the PWRI project had somehow been narrowed to aquifer injectivity rather than to aquifer storage capacity.

Numerous reservoirs in the Gulf of Thailand contain only natural gas. Others contain both oil and a primary gas cap, where the oil is fully saturated with gas and is unable to hold any more at the pressure and temperature of the reservoir. Over geologic time, some gas migrates upward along faults due to its low density, leaving evidence of its trail in the aquifers before occasionally escaping to the ocean floor. Natural gas is highly compressible, providing sufficient storage capacity for PWRI through compression where it occupies only 5 to 10% of the pore space. During more than a year, it was interesting work finding aquifers containing a free gas saturation which were of sufficient size to meet the requirements of a storage site. Once an aquifer candidate was located, simple analytical equations could be used to predict the pressure rise given a volume of PWRI. One day a Chevron technical manager having a geology background came by my desk to say that an edge of the mature Tantawan field had not yet been drilled to test its potential. He had on his desk a recommendation prepared by a Chevron petroleum engineer to basically walk away from the field by releasing its development rights back to the Thai government. A little effort following this hint resulted in a quickly prepared recommendation to drill a well, which was very successful and in turn led to more successful drilling. The field is still producing today. It was good to get away from reservoir simulation and back to operational engineering.

Most Chevron staff live with their young families in the suburbs of Bangkok. They typically have a car and driver on call at all times, but choose to avoid returning to the city on weekends. It was a good work / life balance. We felt free to indulge in weekend travel. Thai Airways flew us to the Four Seasons Resort in Chiang Mai, where we visited a neighboring camp to observe more than one elephant trained to paint a picture by holding a brush in its trunk. That has become a special memory! Thai Airways also flew us to Krabi, a southern province on the Andaman coast where we stayed at Rayavadee, a resort with unique, mushroom-shaped cottages, incredible beaches and limestone outcrops. A car and driver reserved for the occasion drove us 130 miles southeast from Bangkok, where we boarded a speedboat for a short ride to the island of Ko Samet, a national park and home of the recently opened Paradee Resort. When we arrived at the boat dock, there was a coterie of resort staff waiting for us, all in a line and smiling widely. The resort manager, head chef, activities director and support staff were all welcoming us and no others that morning. It was both wonderful and uncomfortable at the same time.

Why is this chapter titled, "Bangkok Buddhism"? There was an overall good feeling living in Bangkok that was not expected. It is a kinder and gentler culture than most others, at least on the surface. My belief is that Buddhism plays a role. When the government of the Prime Minister Thaksin Shinawatra was overthrown by a military coup, armored vehicles were positioned throughout the city. Upon exiting the Mandarin Oriental after lunching with friends, the TS was asked by a smiling hotel bellman, who was glancing at flowers decorating the gun barrel of a Royal Thai Army tank parked nearby, "Taxi or tank, madam?"

CHAPTER SIXTEEN

AS NASTY AS IT GETS

Chevron was one of my best clients and Bangkok was amazing. My contract with them had been preceded by one with the Danes, who strive for hygge and the good life. There were long odds that the next contract would be as good. And it wasn't. The London office of a global energy consulting firm called Knowledge Reservoir (KR) wanted to put me forward for a contract position with Wintershall AG in Moscow. I recall receiving the phone call from KR while in route to the airport in Bangkok, after enjoying a pleasant farewell luncheon with Chevron colleagues. During my first week at home, a second contract position opened; it was with the consulting firm of Fugro-Robertson in Wallingford, England, about 25 miles from Oxford. I quickly arranged two interviews for one trip to Europe, one with Fugro-Robertson, followed by one with Wintershall, at their headquarters in Kassel, Germany. Upon arrival at Heathrow Airport in London, I was met by a Fugro-Robertson driver and driven 40 miles to the small market town of Wallingford, in the upper Thames Valley. I spent the night at the George Hotel, a 16th century coaching inn at the center of town, where it was necessary to stoop when entering the dark public rooms and registration area. Everything about the place and its environs was undersized — even the roads were excessively narrow. The little town contained a few churches and one restaurant. Oxford was a 30 minute drive or a 40 minute train ride, too far for a daily commute. My early impression was not a good one. The interview was scheduled for late the next morning, to allow travel time for two key men driving down from the head office, more than 200 miles away in North Wales. Early in the interview, it became clear that a lot of travel would be required to the Middle East, as their new Chief Reservoir Engineer. That news, combined with the quirky and remote nature of the location, caused me to prematurely stop the interview. There was no reason to continue it. I suggested a return of half the already paid travel expenses for the driver to return me to Heathrow Airport. They were not pleased to accept the offer.

That evening I flew to Frankfurt, Germany, and stayed at the Hilton Airport Hotel, catching a train the next morning to Kassel. Upon my arrival, the memories came flooding back. It was there at Wintershall 25 years earlier where I had first met Ivan de Grisogono, the person who had pointed more business my way than any other, after he moved to Deminex in Essen. And it was there the client had been delivered simulations of reservoir performance that were not finished, as funds allocated for computing had been exhausted. The cast of characters had changed. Only the female reservoir engineer who had been the guest client of Todd, Dietrich & Chase, Inc. remained on staff — or so I thought. There was one other, a petroleum engineer who will surface later in this chronicle, a person who had previously not endorsed my work. The interview went well and I returned to the Frankfurt Hilton Airport Hotel, there to await the written offer that was promised to arrive later that day, directly from Wintershall (WI). But wait! Where was Knowledge Reservoir in this deal? I called the KR agent in London and was stunned to learn that he had not negotiated any contract terms with the Germans. He had done nothing more than arrange the interview. He proposed coming to Frankfurt to present me with a contract that called for my secondment to WI. I asked to see the draft contract. It contained a clause that would prevent me from working with WI for a year, or more, after termination of the project.

That non-standard clause had stopped me from doing business with KR years earlier in Houston. The agent insisted on meeting me at my hotel the next day to discuss a way forward. My position was unchanging — KR would need to negotiate a finder's fee payable by WI and then go their separate way. The project in Moscow was high profile and an important one, involving a new joint venture (JV) between the Russian energy giant Gazprom and WI, for the purpose of supplying natural gas to Germany. It was later learned WI had paid a large lump-sum to eliminate the middleman and secure a contract with me. It was therefore no surprise that my contract with WI would become one of the most profitable of all.

This time the word trailing did not apply to the TS. We traveled together. Our fly date was set by the time needed to obtain our visas at the Russian Consulate in San Francisco, a process that could not begin until a letter of invitation was in-hand from Wintershall in Moscow. It was weeks after signing the contract when we registered at a Marriott Courtyard hotel in Moscow, centrally located near the Tchaikovsky Music Conservatory. In the normal style, the TS found a suitable flat on her own, using the services of a realty company called Penny Lane. The property was owned by a divorced woman who was asking 4,200 dollars per month. It is directly across the street from the Italian Embassy, which occupies a beautiful building called the Berg Villa, built in 1897. Its Red Room was the location where the German Ambassador to Russia was murdered in 1918, only weeks prior to the massacre of the Romanovs. The price was reduced to 3,800 dollars per month when the TS offered to replace the furniture with items and leave them at the end of the contract. The landlady was a character. It was necessary to meet her at our bank monthly, to withdraw and hand her the rent in cash — the equivalent of 3,800 dollars in rubles. She would cram the bills into her purse and walk to a metro, there to catch a train for returning to her dacha, where it was made clear that cocktails for two were on offer whenever the TS was absent from Moscow.

It was a 40-minute walk to the office, along a route that took me near magnificent architecture, including the Cathedral of Christ the Savior on the Moscow River, a few blocks from the Kremlin. The cathedral is the second to stand on its site, completed in the year 2000, as an exact replacement of the original that had been demolished by Stalin. Its reconstruction has been supported by millions of private donations. Images of the rising and setting sun reflecting off that structure are powerfully fixed in my memory. When recalled, they provide a real sense of happiness. Perhaps the remembered sense of euphoria was caused by the release of endorphins and natural high felt while walking rapidly on my commute. Or, more likely, it was simply knowing that another lucrative day was just beginning or ending.

The Russian / German JV is called Achimgaz, an alliance formed to develop a license area of Novy Urengoy, an enormous gas condensate field located 1,600 mi [2,500 km] northeast of Moscow near the Arctic Circle. Upon my arrival in April, 2007, several appraisal wells had been drilled and tests were in progress to determine the productive capacity of the Achimov formation, a low permeability reservoir containing tight gas sands not unlike those of the Soehlingen field in Germany. My position was Consulting Reservoir Engineer, reporting to a Deputy General Director of Drilling, an Austrian newly arrived from drilling wells in the Western Desert of Egypt. With a shaved head, round face, twinkling blue eyes and a wonderful infectious laugh, he brought to mind Elmer Fudd, the Looney Tunes character who is always chasing Bugs Bunny with a shotgun. My job was to estimate how much gas and petroleum liquid (called condensate) might be producible from the reservoir, assuming different field development plans. It was to be a classic application of reservoir simulation. The project team included three young petroleum engineers and three geologists. Each group reported to a different manager, a certain recipe for failure, especially given that neither a project manager nor a principal model architect had been named and empowered by management.

The focus of the JV was on operations, not on field development planning, and certainly not on reservoir simulation. Achimgaz was having problems drilling the appraisal wells, which were called pilot slant wells. The drilling assembly was frequently becoming stuck due to hole collapse upon drilling the last interval of a well. That final section was 600 to 800 feet in length and it was highly deviated — it was nearly horizontal. The Achimov had been penetrated by hundreds of wells in the Western Siberian Basin without problems, but all of them had been drilled mostly vertical, as so-called "S" wells. It was the German member of the JV that wanted to drill nearly horizontally as the well penetrated the oil reservoir to increase its dimensionless productivity index (J_D). However, the production tests were delivering disappointing results. I began thinking about the problem, not as one qualified in the mechanics, but as one knowing about the mathematics of horizontal well productivity. The slant interval was much too short! Analytical solutions available for many years led one to expect a productivity gain of about 10% for the slant wells over the rate from "S" wells. Although problems resulting from slant well drilling had been hugely costly, costing tens of millions of dollars, no one was aware of the marginal benefits associated with this well design. I was amazed when there was no response to this shared explanation for the observed poor well productivity. After all, the Don and Joe Show at Yukos had at least countered with, "We don't believe your results for J_D, prove them."

Aka Elmer Fudd knew little about reservoir modeling and he liked it that way. Without announcing the decision, he gave control to a senior German geologist, who became the de facto project manager. The geologist sequestered himself in an office on a different floor from the remainder of the team and proceeded to build a reservoir model using static data. In an all too frequent manner, as a geologist he ignored critical dynamic data from the production tests. The result was a model delivered after 5 months, which all members of the reservoir engineering team labeled as useless for simulating past and future reservoir performance. Attempts for collaboration between the geology and engineering groups led to nasty rows, made all the worse by visits from a member of the head office staff in Kassel, a person who had been effectively checked by the predecessor of Elmer Fudd. Visiting routinely behind closed doors with the top title in Moscow — the Managing Director — the visitor would weave his web in support of his pals in the geology group. He would dash all efforts to use what are called rock property net / gross (N_{res} / G) ratio arrays in the model building process, resulting in a delivered model that was inconsistent with both the core and flow test information and the degree of heterogeneity described by competitors and published by Russian scientists.

Elmer Fudd finally gave me authority to independently build a model using a structural framework of the reservoir that had been built earlier by a professor at Clausthal University in Germany. I populated the model with rock properties using N_{res} / G ratio arrays and my standard random distribution process. The model gave an initial gas-in-place (GIIP) that was only 38% of the number provided by the WI model. The difference between the two models was enough gas to supply all of Europe for nearly 3 years! When the Managing Director heard the news, he instructed Elmer Fudd to terminate my contract — several weeks early.

Of course I have been curious about what others think of the GIIP in the JV area of Novy Urengoy. Thanks to the Internet, that information is now available. The R&D group of Gazprom is known as TNGG. Located in the Western Siberian city of Tyumen, they have been responsible for designing, developing and operating gas / condensate / oil projects throughout Russia since 1966, many of them in the Achimov. When I left the project, their estimate of GIIP was 280 BSCM. During the period from 2007 to 2015, the JV had drilled 40 wells, most of them with horizontal sections varying in length between 2,000 and 4,000 feet. Data obtained from those wells led TNGG to reduce their estimate from 280 to 200 BSCM — not far above my estimate made 8 years earlier. The JV plans to drill another 60 wells and it is likely there will be another reduction in their estimate of GIIP. The Nord Stream twin pipeline passing through the Baltic Sea was completed in 2011. It began transporting gas from Novy Urengoy to Germany during 2012.

How could a company retain a highly paid consultant and then simply use him as an adjunct to staff? They had shelled out a large lump-sum payment to a search firm and provided more than a competitive daily rate. There had been 10 contracts after 1996, counting the one with Deminex Norge in Oslo. Half of them were upbeat, delivering results that were useful, and leaving both sides open to the possibility of jointly entering future contracts. The other half were negative, failing to deliver anything useful and leaving both sides happy to say goodbye. Why were so many projects ending in failure? It was clear there was a distinction between the good and bad contracts. The bad ones called for a contractor to work as an adjunct to staff, helping where needed and taking direction from the client. The good ones called for independent consulting on a specific project, with a defined scope of work and duration. Why not just take consulting contracts rather than serve as an adjunct to staff? The answer is that fewer contracts were being offered for consultants. Companies wanted their own people to control projects dealing with the subsurface, those that defined the size of the prize — its value and the effect on stock price. That was becoming possible with reservoir simulation technology, given powerful affordable computers and commercially available software. Staff with only a single training course in simulation software were taking the place of the experts from afar. Why not just work under the direction of others and take the money? That's something I had moved away from 30 years earlier when I left Shell Oil Company. There was no going back. I wanted to keep working and we loved the expat life. The adventures were worth the pain! There would be 6 future contracts, all of them full of conflict and ending poorly.

CHAPTER SEVENTEEN

'TWAS ANOTHER SHELL

There are billions of barrels of heavy oil, bitumen and tar beneath the surface of the province of Alberta, Canada. The oil fields have names like Athabasca, Cold Lake and Peace River. When Brent oil prices are in excess of 70 dollars per barrel in today's dollars, the deposits are exploited by surface mining and what are called in-situ recovery techniques, involving the injection of steam to reduce the viscosity of the heavy oil to allow it to flow to production wells. I became more than familiar with these deposits when employed at Shell Development Company. After being on my own in later years, I had worked under contract for Halliburton Energy Services, Inc. on Athabasca and twice for Shell Canada Limited on Peace River. The injection of steam to recover heavy oil was my specialty. The affiliate of Royal Dutch Shell in America was called Shell E&P International, a company headquartered in Houston that served as a think tank to assist subsidiary Shell groups operating outside of the United States, in places like Africa, Canada, The Netherlands and Oman. They did not operate oil fields, they provided company consultants and billed the subsidiaries for their services, as a separate profit center in the overall Shell Group. I had played phone tag with them through the years, never quite connecting on a project before giving them a call when I returned home from Moscow. My timing was perfect. Royal Dutch Shell had just completed buying all of the stock in Shell Canada Limited, with an eye toward full control of their tar sand holdings. Technology needed for exploitation of the tar sands was central for development of heavy oil reservoirs worldwide. Canadians were not happy that efforts were underway to develop and manage their assets by other nationals. As with the Unocal staff in Thailand when it was taken over by Chevron, the integration of Shell Canada and Shell E&P International was not going smoothly. I was again stepping into the middle of an unpleasant power shift.

Following the new business style, Shell outsourced the preparation of my contract to a third party (Collarini Energy Staffing Inc.), after we had agreed to the terms, which included an offer of an expat assignment when one became available in either The Netherlands or Oman. The contract was open-ended, with either party able to terminate without penalty given at least 30-days notice. My job was to screen and rank a series of so-called SAGD (Steam Assisted Gravity Drainage) field pilots as candidates for acquisition. Oil prices were nearing an all-time high and there was an intense global interest in the tar sands. A list of lease holders read like a list of attendees at a United Nations assembly — it included Americans, Canadians, Chinese, French, Germans, Italians and Koreans. The SAGD process relies on a pair of horizontal wells drilled parallel to each other, one directly overlying the other with about 20 feet of vertical separation between the two. The well pair is drilled near the base of a heavy oil sand, and each well is typically 1,500 to 2,000 feet in length, or more. Steam injected into the top well rises to the top of the sand and heated oil drains by gravity to the lower well. The earliest SAGD pilot projects were installed and operated in the Athabasca and Cold Lake oil sands and many of those projects are now mature. Unfortunately, target oil production rates and thermal efficiency (output energy / input energy) have been met in only about 20% of the pilots. The key feature of the underperforming pilots was the assumption of reservoir homogeneity and a lack of awareness concerning the impedance effects caused by the presence of discontinuous shale lenses. The demonstrated intolerance of SAGD to the presence of shale lenses was forewarned by the founder of the process, Roger Butler, when he wrote: "A significant concern in the development of the SAGD process is that of the possible effects of barriers to vertical flow within the reservoir."

While working for Esso Resources Canada Limited in 1978, Butler had designed and directed the first pilot test of SAGD technology. That pilot at Cold Lake preceded the testing of a variant of SAGD in the Kern River field of California, where an early client had drilled horizontal wells from a vertical shaft in 1982. It also preceded the first horizontal well projects installed outside of North America, by Elf Aquitaine in France during 1980 — 1981 and the Institut Francais du Petrole in Italy during 1982. Not only was the late Roger Butler the founder of SAGD, he is widely regarded as the father of horizontal well technology for the global recovery of oil and gas. While on contract to Addax Petroleum in Geneva during 2002, it was surprising to learn they were not aware of mathematics that explained the benefits of drilling horizontal wells parallel to each other. An aerial view of horizontal wells drilled by Addax looked like a pile of pick-up sticks! Butler had moved from Esso to a professorship at the University of Calgary, where he continued with his research on SAGD. I telephoned him from Geneva to ask if he would consider giving an in-house lecture, thinking that the gastronomical delights of that city might attract him. He politely rejected the offer, but remembered me a few years later when he invited me to lunch with him at the University of Calgary faculty dining room. Given my interest in horizontal well productivity that had earned me a best paper award in 1996, we were able to carry on a good technical conversation. This was another example of when a publication and a dime resulted in something more than a cup of coffee; in this case it earned a fine lunch with a distinguished industry leader.

The new project aimed toward acquisition of prime SAGD acreage was highly confidential. Half of the 12-person team were located in Calgary and half in Houston. All reported to a young Manager of New Ventures, a highly ambitious type who held a MS degree in structural geology. Nearly all other team members were also geologists or well log analysts. Failure of the first horizontal well steam pilot in the United States had been caused by the impedance effects of a shale lens on the gravity drainage of hot oil. I had become interested in the effects of shale at that time and had an idea of how to predict and avoid areas which were likely to result in poor SAGD performance, prior to investing tens of millions of dollars for development. The project gave the chance to test my conceptual model using reservoir simulation and publicly available data from real field performance. The results showed that shale lenses occupying only 5% of the bulk volume are capable of reducing the vertical permeability of a homogeneous and isotropic reservoir by two to three orders of magnitude, or more. In a practical sense, this meant that at Athabasca and Cold Lake, it is only the bitumen and heavy oil occurring within the least heterogeneous, multiply-stacked channel sands that are likely to be exploited commercially with a SAGD process. And not much acreage is underlain by a series of stacked channel sands in Alberta.

Key geologists assigned to the project were exploration geologists. They were good scientists and generalists trained to find petroleum reservoirs, not to describe the geology of a specific reservoir once it had been found. Skill sets required to understand the presence and distribution of shale lenses seemed to be missing among the Shell team members. What are called production or development geologists, or geological engineers, were available within Shell, but the project leadership was unaware of their need. From the outset, I called repeatedly for what is known as a shaly sand analysis of the reservoirs, using techniques published by researchers at Shell Development Company 30 years earlier. Most of the staff were ignorant of the approach. They refused to consider its application, notwithstanding the fact that the shaly sand methodology was in worldwide use and it had been specifically developed for application to Peace River. They needed to defend the techniques they had been using for years. Not only was shaly sand analysis capable of detecting the presence of thin shale lenses, it raised other awareness. When it was demonstrated that its application gave a 15% lift in the calculation of initial bitumen-in-place as compared to the conventional analysis, senior management stepped-in and forced the staff to change their methods. It didn't matter whether I was providing favorable or unfavorable results for a company. Either way, there was nearly always contentious pushback that most often came from geologists.

Shortly after my arrival at Shell in April, 2008, West Texas Intermediate (WTI) oil had reached an all-time high price (adjusted for inflation) of $152 per barrel. Nine months later, it had fallen to $46 per barrel. It was the sub-prime mortgage crisis in the United States that triggered the global recession and led to the price collapse. The project was suspended and I was transferred to a fresh SAGD project called Orion near Cold Lake. Phase 1 of the project had been installed, consisting of 22 SAGD well pairs. It was delivering 4,500 barrels per day of heavy oil into a central facility designed to handle 10,000 barrels per day. An additional 24 well pairs were planned for Phase 2 and more for a Phase 3. It was clear that Phase 1 had been placed in the best portion of the lease — Phases 2 and 3 would be developing areas with higher concentrations of shale lenses. After three months of evaluation, my simple calculations showed the hot oil would drain very slowly at non-commercial rates as it cascaded downward through the series of shale baffles to the SAGD production wells. I recommended a full stop of all activity beyond Phase 1, potentially impacting a team of 20 to 30 staff members in Calgary and Houston. The project manager was livid, complaining to senior management and refusing to endorse payment for any more of my services on Orion.

About that same time, it was officially announced that all expat rotations within Shell would be eliminated within 1 to 2 years, as an austerity measure during the global economic downturn. Expats comprised 20 to 30% of the Shell E&P International staff. It was costly to load up their household goods in containers, pay an allowance for local housing, fly all family members in business class and ship the family pets around the globe. There would no longer be a chance for us to work as Shell expats in overseas locations. That news was actually not distressing. We were well on our way towards moving to a different contract, one with BP at their North Sea Headquarters in Dyce, Scotland, a suburb of Aberdeen. Upon referral from a colleague well known to me from the days of Yukos, the petroleum consultancy of AGR TRACS International had set up a telephone interview for me with Nigel Herbert, a reservoir engineering team leader at BP. All parties were shocked when it was verbally agreed at the end of the 30-minute call that the job was mine. I was immediately on-board — Nigel was atypical and that was interesting. He was an elder, an intellectual, a man with a sense of humor and he played violin in the Aberdeen Chamber Orchestra. Working as an adjunct to his staff might not be so bad. The job offer was made quickly, presumably on the basis of good marks given from BP staff who knew me and my currently active employment on an open-ended contract with Shell.

There was one high hurdle to get over before landing in Aberdeen. As a citizen of a country not belonging to the European Union, I needed a permit to work in the UK. The first step was to be sponsored by a company registered in the UK. As the agent ready to handle the administration of my contract for a fee of 20%, or more, of my compensation, TRACS was keen to sponsor me. In fact, they were willing to do more than sponsor: They agreed to retain a legal firm specializing in Immigration Law and pay the funds required to secure a so-called Tier 1 (General) Highly Skilled Migrant Work Permit, offered under a short-lived, points-based permitting system that was later closed to overseas applicants in 2010. An applicant earned points for proof of cash on-hand, prospective salary, educational degree held, proficiency in English and other measures. He needed to exceed a minimum number of points to obtain the permit. The amount of required detail sent by overseas-courier to Gillian Brownlee, a Chartered Legal Executive at the law firm of Kingsley Napley LLP in London was incredible. Based on scoring a high number of points, we took a chance and terminated the Shell contract before signing a contract with TRACS. While driving across West Texas on our return to California, a call came in from the UK Immigration Service. The caller waited patiently while I pulled off the interstate where a speed of 90 mph was the norm. She wanted verbal assurance of provided key information before saying the permit had been approved.

Once again, I became curious when writing this chronicle about my views that often ran counter to those of the client personnel. Was I basically an obstructionist, looking to prove others wrong, wanting and needing to be the smartest one in the room? Or was there really a need to blow the whistle? Searching the Internet reveals that Shell eventually understood the need to stop development of the Orion project. Although they received approval to install Phase 2 from the government of Alberta, it was not installed, and 5 years after my departure Shell sold the lease to Osum Oil Sands, the operator of an adjacent property. Orion had been on the market for more than 2 years before the buyer was found. Osum has now filled the capacity of the production facility by injecting more steam to produce the oil, incurring reduced thermal efficiency and increased operating costs in the process. It's now 8 years following my departure. Although WTI oil prices have averaged 100 dollars per barrel for nearly half of this time period, Phase 2 has not yet been installed. Osum has publicly declared that any future SAGD well pairs will need to be placed very carefully to avoid the effects of shale lenses.

CHAPTER EIGHTEEN

YELLOW PEAFLOWERS

It was late November, 2008, when I arrived in Aberdeen, the oil hub of Europe. The cold, fresh air was bracing and a welcome from the atmosphere of Houston. The city was smaller than expected, with a single high street and a population of only 200,000. There were seagulls overhead and beautiful granite buildings everywhere.

I found the Brentwood Hotel perfectly located and its 3 stars in need of polishing. Its mostly male guests were rendezvousing before flying offshore for work shifts on the North Sea oil platforms. It was only minutes in the bar before I was politely told that discussing oil business at the hotel was off limits. Working offshore was dangerous. Helicopter crashes were not rare, nor were deadly accidents on the platforms. The men wanted to enjoy terra firma and relax as long as possible without talking about work. Before arrival of the TS a few days later, it had become clear that the hotel was pretty grim. Alternatives were either remotely located on the edge of town, filled with no vacancy or very expensive. At the end of the Shell contract, TRACS had paid the early termination penalty at our high rise apartment and the cost of shipping a car back to California. Given that negotiated coverage, I had not pushed for full reimbursement of temporary living expenses in Aberdeen. We quickly began the search for a residence and settled on one in the Ferryhill area, near Duthie Park and the banks of the River Dee. It was one of the downstairs units in an old 2-story granite home that had been converted into a residential quadraplex. The place was small, furnished and comfortable.

The North Sea Headquarters of BP are reachable via a 10 minute, non-stop train ride from the central Aberdeen train station. My daily one-way commute consisted of the train ride plus 2 walking segments, each of 15 minutes duration. It was almost always dark and often wet during my commute. Aberdeen is at nearly the same latitudes as Oslo and Moscow, but the winter weather in those cities was less difficult to tolerate. The difference was quiet snowfall versus rain driven sideways by the North Sea wind. BP staff work on what's called a 9/80 schedule, meaning they work 80 hours over 9 days rather than the traditional 10 days. This schedule is also known as a Flex Friday program. While in Geneva on contract with Addax, we had rented a car for use on occasional weekends. A personal car had not been needed there, nor in any other of our expat locations. With every other Friday off and so much to see in Scotland, we decided to buy a car. The TS chose a used Peugeot 307. Before long she was smoothly driving on the left, shifting the manual transmission with her left hand and negotiating frequent roundabouts, all while traveling along unfamiliar roads, occasionally on ice and snow. The car served us well. It was easily sold at the end of the contract by advertising it on the BP digital bulletin board.

We got to know many castle hotels and manor houses on the 3-day weekends. They were relaxing with huge, wood burning fireplaces and quiet library rooms, where we often played the board game *Scrabble*™ and occasionally read. We celebrated Christmas at a Georgian manor house on the River Dee, 20 miles west of Aberdeen, at a place called Banchory Lodge. We chatted fireside in the lounge with the only other registered couple on Christmas Eve and had a bay window table for two at Christmas lunch, in a dining room with nearly a hundred locals present in family groups.

In the standard manner, there was no welcoming upon our arrival in Aberdeen. However, in this case we were invited to a Sunday afternoon performance of the Aberdeen Chamber Orchestra, where the client violinist introduced himself during the intermission. Nigel Herbert was as I imagined — reserved, bespectacled, of slight build and overqualified for his job as a reservoir engineering team leader. The next morning he introduced me to his team and defined my job description. The team consisted of 4 geologists and 2 reservoir engineers. I was replacing one of the engineers who was a contractor from LR Senergy, a global energy services consultancy with headquarters in Aberdeen. The other engineer was a legacy employee with a PhD who had worked in BP's Sunbury-On-Thames research center. Upon our introduction, he proudly announced that he knew nothing about reservoir simulation and liked it that way. I found it strange that the spouses, ex-spouses or partners of four of the team members were either also working in the head office of BP, or in the local office of TRACS. That had not been allowed in any other client office, owing to conflict of interest and confidentiality concerns. The ex-spouse of the PhD regularly visited the open working area to coordinate childcare duties, sharing, without knowing, more than anyone wanted to hear.

17. View of Lake Geneva and the Alps from the terrace dining room of
Hotel Victoria Glion in Montreux, Switzerland.

18. Hotel Victoria Glion is even more beautiful when draped in snow.

19. Old Benedictine monastery next to Lake Annecy called Abbaye de Talloires, now a hotel.

20. Lake Annecy is claimed to be the cleanest lake in Europe, owing to stringent environmental laws imposed in the 1960s.

21. The Sommelier at the restaurant in Hotel Abbaye de Talloires was scolding when I emptied red wine too close to the bottom of the bottle in his absence.

22. The Moscow River and Kremlin taken from the windows of our 8th story flat.

23. The Admiral Hotel on the wharf in Copenhagen, a few blocks from the
Maersk office building.

24. View of the Copenhagen Opera House from our room
in the Admiral Hotel.

25. The Maersk flagship building in Copenhagen with the 7-pointed white star on the blue background logo shown in upper left of the photo.

26. Sirocco on the 64th floor of Lebua State Tower in Bangkok, the world's highest outdoor restaurant and bar, just "upstairs" from our 24th-floor serviced apartment.

27. Sirocco is no place for those afflicted by acrophobia.

28. The Tchaikovsky Music Conservatory in central Moscow
near our apartment.

29. Even the aisles would become filled with seated patrons at the Tchaikovsky Music Conservatory.

30. The Italian Embassy in Moscow occupies this building called the Berg Villa built in 1897. Our apartment was located directly across the street with this view from the master bedroom window.

31. The Red Room of Berg Villa where the German Ambassador
to Russia was murdered in 1918.

32. Cathedral of Christ the Savior on the Moscow River, a few blocks from the Kremlin, was passed on my daily walks to-and-from the office.

33. Banchory Lodge on the River Dee, 20 miles west of Aberdeen, Scotland.

34. The hills were resplendent with the color of yellow gorse and broom
in Scotland.

The focus of the project was Wytch Farm, Europe's largest onshore oil field, located in southern England. It had been the jewel in the crown of BP for more than 30 years. It was time to update the reservoir model that had been built 5 years earlier. My mandate was clearly defined. It was to ensure full reservoir engineering engagement with the new static model build and to perform dynamic modeling in support of the water injection strategy. The questions were, "How much oil is remaining in the reservoir, 'Where is it', and 'How much can be recovered by either drilling additional wells or changing the water injection program?'" Upon my arrival, the local office of TRACS was already working with BP to find infill drilling locations and to calculate likely volumes of recoverable oil. They needed to convince BP and its partners that a proposed well would be profitable. BP owned 67.8% of the field and operated it. Its partners were Premier (12.4%), Maersk (7.4%), Summit (7.4%) and Talisman (5.0%). In jointly owned operations, technical committee meetings (TCMs) are held at regular intervals wherein the operator updates partners with operational results and future plans. While attending my first TCM on Wytch Farm, one of the partners voiced, "Frankly, the feeling is that calculations are skewed to the high side to get the well approved." This was an echo of a comment privately made to me by the Senergy reservoir engineer during our brief overlap. When hearing presentations by TRACS staff in support of drilling, I had the feeling they were under pressure to either justify a proposed well or risk losing the BP contract. The sniff of scotch whiskey too early on the presentation days was telling.

This was going to be a tough slog. My technical work needed to be aligned with the concepts of both BP and TRACS. A triple dose of more bad news was on its way. My virtuoso team leader would be playing his violin elsewhere within BP. He was being replaced by a geologist who was returning from maternity leave on a part time basis. She and her husband had coordinated their work schedules at BP to share the parenting duty. It was all like a big group hug, incestuous, without the coziness of Danish hygge. The next event was more troubling. Oil prices had reached an inflation adjusted record low, prompting BP to demand that TRACS and all other vendors reduce their prices by 15%. I shared the pain, agreeing with TRACS to a 7.5% decrease in my daily compensation rate. This marked only the second time in more than 30 years that my invoices would not be paid in full. The first was when a private entrepreneur paid 90% on the dollar after declaring bankruptcy. In this case, BP was a publicly traded company that was reportedly continuing to pay bonuses to top management during the down turn. The final unpleasant news quickly followed — the Wytch Farm project would be cancelled, contractors terminated and all staff reassigned at year-end, which was eight months away.

My immediate concern was how to align with results being delivered by the local TRACS office. There had been reason for unease before signing the contract with them. As the advisors to Addax in Geneva, TRACS had supported drilling horizontal wells without regard to azimuth, revealing ignorance about the benefits of parallel well placement. Now, at Wytch Farm, other alarms were sounding. TRACS were claiming that all oil producible by a new infill well would add proven reserves. Ignoring standard practice, they were not subtracting oil that would have been produced by the offsetting, active wells, absent the drilling of a new well. Perhaps they were artificially improving the reserves replacement ratio (RRR), a metric often used to award compensation to top management via a bonus pool. And then there was the issue of the Scottish bag pipes. The major reservoir at Wytch Farm consists of a series of alternating layers of sandstones and mud-rich sediments that had been interpreted as mudstones. In previous models, mudstones were considered to form field-wide probable seals. Fluid movement through these zones is required in some areas of the field to explain observed field performance. The standard interpretation had been that natural fractures are present that cut-through the seals, thereby providing the necessary inter-zone communication. TRACS had bizarrely introduced the use of pipe-flow routines (pipes) to simulate fluid flow through fractures, never mind that fractures had not been observed in the vast amount of recovered core material. Moreover, pipe-flow routines are codes developed for modeling the mechanics of fluid flow through surface pipelines or wellbores. Their use in this application was seemingly unprecedented and appeared to be an ad-hoc, desperate attempt to reproduce observed reservoir performance without understanding the geology. The violinist was heading another team elsewhere in the office building. When I sought his counsel on the need for alignment with TRACS, he privately suggested that I play solo, rather than as part of the orchestra.

Alignment with BP was a different issue, made more difficult by an internal modeling philosophy called Top Down Reservoir Modeling (TDRM). Basically calling for the use of simple, coarse models rather than detailed ones,

TDRM is a proprietary technology developed by BP. One of its inventors was also working in the Dyce office, where a detailed reservoir model of Wytch Farm had never been built. The full-field model (FFM) in use by BP divided the reservoir into 62,000 grid cells, with different rock properties assigned to each cell. In the current project, we were building a FFM that divided the reservoir into 1,400,000 grid cells! Halfway through the project, resident authors of TDRM lobbied their managers to stop building a FFM, contending that not enough data were in hand to warrant proceeding with such a detailed reservoir description. At that same time, I happened to pose a question that probably resulted in continuation of my contract employment — a good thing, since mild spring and summer weather was on its way, promising a series of enjoyable three-day weekends. Given pressure measurements in the mudstones that were declining over time, how could these rocks be impermeable and acting as seals? A light bulb began burning in the mind of the lead geologist who was acting as the principal model architect. He arranged for a specialist at the University of Aberdeen to study core samples taken of the inferred mudstone intervals. I was invited to a workshop at the core storage facility and to a presentation of the findings given at BP by Professor Colin North. I sat in the audience listening to a very professional talk that discredited interpretations of the geology long held by BP and TRACS. It was difficult to not look smug. The so-called mudstones were actually siltstones and fine-grained sandstones with highly variable secondary porosity and permeability formed by diagenesis. Using multiple layers to represent each of these intervals and a random distribution of rock properties within each layer, sufficient connectivity was established in the detailed model to allow inter-zone fluid movement. There was no need for modeling open natural fractures that had not been seen in the core material. And there was no longer a need for holding onto zany, pipe flow concepts!

Neither the team leader nor her lead geologist initially supported my modeling approach that resulted in a series of equi-probable reservoir descriptions. I was told that BP preferred a single, deterministic view of what lay below the surface. When I pointed out that my methods were aligned with those presently in use by BP at Prudhoe Bay in Alaska, they began to listen. The open-minded lead geologist eventually accepted my proposed techniques and explained them to the team leader. He later presented them with vigor at a TCM meeting with partners.

The Scottish countryside was always filled with the color yellow. Used to produce a vegetable oil, rapeseed is bright yellow and cultivated fields of it were everywhere, causing us to stop often along the roadside to snap yet another picture. Even more beautiful were the wild evergreen shrubs of gorse and broom, both displaying rich, yellow peaflowers that produce a distinctive coconut scent, especially when wet. The two are equally stunning, differing mostly in their degree of thorniness. The stems of broom are long, flexible and smooth, whereas gorse stems are spiky — dangerously so. It's claimed that a hiker slipping off a trail and falling into a thicket of gorse actually had to be vertically lifted off of the thorns by helicopter! We have no recall of spikes pulling at our clothes when walking through the yellow hills. It must have been broom that provided our sensory overload.

During the final stage of the project, I was allowed to work independently with the big FFM. The dynamic simulations indicated that recently drilled wells were mostly accelerating oil production — they were recovering oil that would have been produced anyway from surrounding wells. That was the bad news. The good news was that pockets of remaining oil had been pinpointed where wells drilled in the future might recover additional reserves. Moreover, the volume of original oil-in-place had been underestimated, meaning that more oil would ultimately be producible than planned. I wrote a final report and distributed it to BP as a locked digital file. It could be read, but not edited without a password. That night, while dining at a restaurant in Aberdeen with the TS, my cell phone rang. It was the Director of TRACS. He was calling to say that BP wanted no mention of acceleration in the report. Of course! How obtuse of me. Perhaps that would mean reserves already added as proven would need to be removed from BP's books. And there was no incentive or mechanism for clawing back bonuses that may already have been awarded on the basis of reserve additions. Rewriting the report to remove its essence was not possible, yet TRACS would not pay my final invoices without compliance. What to do? The solution that had worked in the Elk Hills equity dispute came to mind. There, the U.S. Department of Energy needed to discredit my report because they were unhappy with its results (Chapter 6). They refused to pay invoices until all project files, including confidential material provided by Chevron, had been released to their consultants. A simple solution became clear after months of handwringing. Payment was received after all project files were placed in boxes and forwarded directly to the U.S. Secretary of Energy, for her handling. At Wytch Farm, the matter was resolved when it was agreed that I would send TRACS an unlocked digital file of the report for their handling, given the condition that my name was removed from it.

BP may be a different oil company when it comes to safety. It's not the little safety things. There's a fanatical focus on those, like receiving a yellow card for failing to hold onto the handrail when traversing stairs, or failing to back your automobile into its employee parking space. Every employee is expected to monitor his fellows and issue a "gotcha" at least once a year. BP is different because of the number and size of its big safety issues. The Macondo well blowout in the Gulf of Mexico occurred in April, 2010, four months after the end of our contract, resulting in the deaths of 11 men and unprecedented damage to the environment. BP was cited with gross negligence and reckless conduct, ultimately paying 18.7 billion dollars in fines, the largest corporate settlement in history. That disaster had been preceded 5 years earlier by an explosion at the Texas City Refinery owned by BP, in which 15 men lost their lives and 170 were injured. Cost cutting and pressure to raise production were cited as the principal causes of that calamity.

Shortly after our departure, BP sold its majority share of the Wytch Farm oil field to the Anglo-French company Perenco and its Texas City Refinery to Marathon Oil in 2011, to pay a portion of its fines related to the Gulf of Mexico oil spill. Perenco now registers proven oil reserves for Wytch Farm that appear to have been taken directly from my final report — for oil producible from new wells drilled into the pockets of oil defined using detailed reservoir modeling. The hyped TDRM approach apparently had been incapable of finding those jewels, in what had been the crown of BP.

CHAPTER NINETEEN

KHOI IN VIETNAM

My office phone rang several months after returning home from BP and Aberdeen. The caller was George Hepler, the Group Engineering Director for SOCO International Plc., an independent oil company headquartered in London and listed on the London Stock Exchange. Hepler had worked for Conoco in Houston when Todd, Dietrich & Chase Inc. were in their heyday. He was calling to offer a position with SOCO in Ho Chi Minh City (formerly Saigon), working as a Deputy Subsurface Manager. That sounded like an interesting venture, one where I would have control of both the geology and reservoir engineering functions. It was April, 2010, when I arrived there, thinking on my flight about the irony of it all. I had entered the oil industry 44 years earlier to avoid the military draft and deployment to Vietnam. By helping produce energy for ships and planes, I was absent the military and employed at Shell Oil Company with what was called a critical skills deferment. Now, I was entering Vietnam to help them produce energy for their unaltered communist regime, after they had won what they called the American War.

It had taken several weeks to mobilize, a process that required obtaining multiple-entry visas, immunizations, and documents confirming there had been no criminal activity of record. I was met the morning after registering at the Sheraton Hotel by an employee of SOCO, who was serving as the Deputy General Manager of the Hoang Long Joint Operating Company (JOC). His name was Vincent (aka Vinny), an Irishman who had lived in Vietnam for 10 years with his Vietnamese wife and children. Upon meeting in the hotel lobby, he said, "Lose the sportcoat," and I instantly liked him. We walked a few blocks together to the office as he chain smoked and described the venture. SOCO held the controlling interest in the Te Giac Trang (TGT) field, located in the Cuu Long Basin beneath the South China Sea. TGT is also called the White Rhinoceros field. It was not scheduled to begin production until 2015, after 2 offshore platforms were in place and 16 wells had been drilled. White Rhino is operated by the JOC, a partnership owned by PetroVietnam (PV), SOCO, PTT Exploration & Production (PTT) and OPECO. PV in turn is wholly owned by the Vietnamese central government and PTT is a subsidiary of the state-owned public utility company of Thailand. There were lots of disparate owners, all working chaotically together in the same office complex. I was replacing a petroleum engineer who had resigned in frustration after less than 2 years as the prior Deputy Subsurface Manager.

When I politely asked to see an organogram to learn about the structure of the organization, none was forthcoming. I would be reporting to Dung, the Subsurface Manager and a member of the communist party representing the interests of PetroVietnam. But wait! Who was this other person reporting to Dung, also with the title of Deputy Subsurface Manager? Her name was Jang, a Thai national representing the interests of PTT. The position that had been offered to me was actually one of Co-Deputy Subsurface Manager! The title, in itself, was not important, never mind that Jang had been honing her relationships and defining her turf for more than a year. Other troubles were on the way.

The first difficulty was revealed at a meeting held to select well locations for the initial drilling program. A geophysicist who had previously worked for Conoco had been given complete control of where to place the wells. It was clear that although he was a subsurface specialist, he did not report to the Subsurface Manager (Dung), or to either of his Deputy Subsurface Managers (Jang or myself). He reported to the Exploration Manager for SOCO who resided in Calgary, Alberta, Canada. The wells were being positioned at locations based on consideration of only geological concepts, without regard for the dynamics of fluid flow. There was no planning for how a well would fit into a future pattern layout that would likely be needed for water injection to maintain reservoir pressure. There were also no estimates of oil recovery provided for the proposed wells. When I raised these points during the presentation, they were not understood and ignored. The second difficulty was associated with the on-going reservoir model building process. Once again, a geologist was deciding the methodology without collaborating with the reservoir engineering group. This was not unexpected, but as a Deputy Subsurface Manager, it was surprising to learn that changing the status quo would be necessary. A power struggle ensued and when it was settled weeks later, my mandate was the supervision and mentorship of 4 Vietnamese reservoir engineers, and no others. The Exploration Manager had been with SOCO since its inception. He had close family ties with the Canadian geologist who was building the reservoir model of White Rhino. The battle was lost before it began.

Life in Ho Chi Minh City is very high energy and fascinating. Stunning French colonial architecture is all over the place. At the same time, it was understood why Hepler lived in Portland, Oregon, and the Exploration Manager lived in Calgary, both making quarterly visits to the office in Vietnam. It was a difficult place for family life. It was hot and humid. Schooling was a problem and the motorbike traffic congestion was intolerable. Using the LinkedIn^{TM} website when writing this, I learned that the project geologist and geophysicist had both left SOCO and Ho Chi Minh City before White Rhino came on production. They were family men and life was probably less difficult elsewhere. It seems only Vinny with the Vietnamese wife and family stayed the course.

In the usual manner, we insisted on choosing our own housing for the contract. We viewed three options and quickly picked the Intercontinental Hotel. It was new, on the 15th floor, with a balcony offering great views of the city and its military marching bands. The space was more lavish than any other we had occupied in our expat living. Khoi was our driver. He lived with his wife and young son an hour outside of the city. Each day he commuted round trip by motorbike to a garage where he transferred to the company car. After driving me to the office, he was on-duty for the TS the remainder of the day. When not needed, he sat roadside and played a type of mahjong with his pals.

Why had SOCO offered the position of a second Deputy Subsurface Manager? The subsurface interests of PetroVietnam and PTT were both represented by the serving Manager and his Deputy — a second Deputy was needed to represent the views of SOCO. More importantly, my mandate was set by SOCO. Why was it limited to supervising four Vietnamese reservoir engineers, not one of whom wanted to learn English? The answer was clear. A triumvirate of SOCO geologists were in control of establishing the reserve base and, therefore, the value of White Rhino. With close personal ties to management, why would they cede power to a newcomer in a revised organizational structure?

There is a favorite maxim of former consultants who are now working as adjuncts to staff in a work style that has become the norm in the petroleum industry — "We take two empty buckets along to a new contract, money goes in one and manure in the other. When either bucket is full, it's time to go home." Money had always been a concern. A pension and living the expat life as a consultant were mutually exclusive. At the same time, it was not possible to simply take the money and yield control of the reservoir model building to others. The JOC had spent a lot of money getting us to Ho Chi Minh City and signing a long-term lease with the Intercontinental Hotel. In an effort to keep it all going, I made the case for imposing a standard organizational structure within SOCO. The insights of HS were sent in writing to the Deputy Chief Executive Officer in London, the man who had signed my contract for SOCO. The response from one Deputy to another was delivered verbally by Vinny: "That little Co-Deputy will agree to contract termination without recourse, or face legal action." A few days later, Khoi had not been made available to drive us to the airport. There was no question about which bucket had reached its fill point first.

CHAPTER TWENTY

BAREFOOT BEDOUINS

There were just two locations in the Middle East that were of interest for another expat living adventure: the United Arab Emirates (UAE) was one and Oman was the other. A Regional Manager for Senergy Resources Ltd., a global energy services consultancy headquartered in Aberdeen, Scotland, called during July, 2010. Stuart Walley was unknown and calling from Dubai, the most populous of the seven United Arab Emirates, which are a federation of hereditary absolute monarchies on the Arabian Gulf. He was offering a contract position with the Abu Dhabi Company for Onshore Petroleum Operations Ltd. (ADCO), owned by the Emirate of Abu Dhabi, which is ruled by the Al Nahyan royal family. Walley was masterful in presenting the case for accepting an 18-month contract, working in Abu Dhabi on Bu Hasa, one of the 20 largest oil fields in the world. ADCO was acting as operator, holding 60% of the asset. BP, ExxonMobil, Shell and Total each held a 9.5% interest and a Portuguese company (Partex) held the remaining 2%, forming a split that had been in place for more than 70 years. The best and the brightest employees of the major shareholding companies were said to be working on a new project. ADCO needed to match the expertise of the foreign specialists and Senergy was offering to provide them with adjuncts to staff. The phone call was unusual for several reasons: It was a Saturday, which is the second day of the weekend in Muslim countries and a curious time for a business call; the clarity of thought and crisp, intelligent English of the caller were different; and then there was a keen interest in my candidacy and a sense of urgency, as though a response of, "Not interested," would not be acceptable to the caller. All was later clarified when I learned that a former colleague at Intercomp, known 32 years earlier, had been seconded to ADCO as an ExxonMobil key employee. He had seen my resume in a big stack of them and had lobbied for my recruitment.

It was ironic that the date of my inaugural arrival in the Middle East was September 11th! On my flight was a long, lean Texan, sprawled with legs outstretched in a business class seat with his Stetson pulled low, covering his eyes for the duration of the flight. He looked like Clint Eastwood in The Good, the Bad and the Ugly, short the Toscano cigar and a holstered six-gun. It was clear he was returning from a rotational break that was part of a common work style in the petroleum industry, one involving 6 to 8 weeks of daily work followed by 3 weeks of rest. His body language said it all — he was irritated. He did not want to be returning to a camp in the desert, where he would continue drilling wells or supervising a field crew. He was most likely an employee, without the option of leaving a contract when either the money or crap bucket reached its fill point. The wretched looking Texan was a reminder that even serving as an adjunct to staff had its advantages, especially given the favorable contract signed with Senergy. In addition to an attractive daily rate for engineering services, we were reimbursed for temporary hotel living expenses, we had an annual housing allowance, a one-time furniture allowance, a monthly transportation allowance and a daily per diem. And most significantly, there would be no income taxes owed to the United Arab Emirates while working under the contract.

Abu Dhabi is both an Emirate and a city, famous for its Corniche, a paved path running more than 5 miles along the waterfront of a bay on the Arabian Gulf. It was a difficult housing market — residential construction had stopped at the time of the 2008 financial crisis and, although the building freeze had thawed, the return of increasing numbers of expats was occurring faster than the previously stalled projects could be completed. It was simply good fortune when the TS learned of an American couple whose business contract had not been renewed. They were returning to California upon short notice. Their space became our space along with 2/3 of their furniture. The flat was located on the 21st floor of Golden Beach Tower, on the Corniche, overlooking the bay and Lulu Island, a breakwater sheltering Abu Dhabi from the open waters of the Arabian Gulf. Floor to ceiling operable windows ran the length of the living room, providing views of the Corniche and water with its myriad of sail boats, enjoyed by many guests during our residency. The location was perfect — it allowed walking 40 minutes along the Corniche to the ADCO offices early most mornings, before the onset of high heat, nearly year-round. The return was less pleasant, requiring removal of a necktie at the beginning and cold showering upon reentry to the flat. The recent financial crash had seen a sudden, mass exodus from the UAE. Those leasing vehicles and residential property had simply broken their contracts, leaving the keys and a sea of cars in the long term parking lot of the Dubai airport. Later it has become necessary to pay the housing lease fees in advance, either in one annual or two semi-annual installments. Senergy paid a single lump sum to the Emirati owners of the flat as our allowance, and we supplemented it with an additional 10% to satisfy the annual fee.

My desk was on the 5th floor of the ADCO building. It was an open work environment, without partitions, where 40, or more, petroleum engineers and earth scientists worked side-by-side. There again was a feeling of a United Nations assembly. The project team consisted of 12 members, from Algeria, America, Egypt, Germany, Indonesia, Pakistan, Palestine, Scotland, Syria, Tunisia and the UAE. Desks nearest the view windows were occupied by the Subsurface Manager of Bu Hasa, the Project Manager, a Chief Geologist and several senior Emiratis heading other projects. The Subsurface Manager reported to an Emirati Vice President, who occupied a private corner office with incredible views of the Arabian Gulf. The mix of various national groups within the team echoed the diversity within the UAE: Only 16% of the total population are Emiratis, mostly Sunni Muslims, 8% are westerners, and the bulk of the remainder are Indians and Bangladeshis. On my first day, I was kept waiting in the building lobby by Security Services until the TS arrived with a necktie, which when worn with a short or long-sleeved shirt without a coat met the standard for expats and allowed access beyond the reception area. The Emirati men wore more of a costume than practical clothing — an ankle length white cotton or wool kandura; a white cotton scarf called a keffiyeh, worn indoors and out, and secured to the head by a pliable band called agal; and open-toed leather sandals. Only Emiratis were allowed to wear their national dress in the office; all others were expected to wear western style clothing. It was awkward in the men's rooms when adjustments were needed to headgear that had gone awry during prayer. Then, it seemed best to look straight ahead into the mirrors to avoid eye contact, especially if the tweaking was being done by a Vice President.

Bu Hasa is classified as a super giant field, holding more than 20 billion barrels of oil in-place. It's the jewel in the keffiyeh. The field is heart-shaped, 22 miles long and up to 13 miles wide. It began producing in 1965 and shortly reached a designed plateau oil production rate of 600,000 barrels per day. The operating philosophy is to maintain the plateau for as long as possible before ultimately recovering 60% of the total oil-in-place, an upper limit that is unlikely to be reached given current technology. Upon my arrival, about 25% of the oil in-place had been recovered. Water injection was started in 1973 to support the reservoir pressure that had been naturally declining in response to the withdrawal of oil. In what became the first of several major operating gaffes, ADCO chose to install a peripheral water injection scheme rather than a pattern waterflood, simply replicating what was being done in Saudi Arabia and Kuwait. Over time, peripheral injection has been shown to be incapable of maintaining reservoir pressure in the heart of the field, where hundreds of wells have been drilled to stay on the plateau. The field is just too big to support the pressure by injecting along its edges. It had become necessary to shut-in many wells to prevent the reservoir pressure from falling below the bubble-point pressure — the level below which natural gas begins to come out of solution in the oil. When operating below bubble-point, a two-phase water and oil reservoir system quickly becomes a three-phase system, and highly mobile gas will run out of control, breaking through to oil wells and changing them into gas wells. An oil production capacity of 50,000 barrels per day had been shut-in to prevent falling below the bubble-point pressure. The only solution for improved operations is to change the peripheral injection scheme to a pattern layout, in a process that calls for drilling many new wells and building a new water injection distribution system. In essence, the field needs to be redeveloped.

There was a second major problem. After several decades, injected water had begun to break through to the production wells, rendering them incapable of flowing the mixture of oil and water that had suddenly become heavier than oil alone. It's standard practice in the oil industry to install either pumping or gas-lift equipment in production wells to prepare them for handling water that is inevitably produced with the oil. It was surprising that ADCO had not been ready for the water! They had simply been replacing wells that would no longer flow with new wells drilled in areas temporarily devoid of injected water, as a means of maintaining the overall plateau rate. An additional oil production capacity of 30,000 barrels per day had been shut-in until artificial lift equipment could be installed in wet wells that would no longer flow naturally.

Employees of the major shareholders (SH) called for fixes at microphones, in a series of annual, formal meetings held on the top floor of the ADCO office complex, where 60, or more, men and several women sat facing a head table holding representatives of the controlling ownership: the Abu Dhabi National Oil Company (ADNOC), ADCO and a Sheik or two from the Al Nahyan royal family. ADCO had been operating the field since its discovery in 1962. It's said they had repeatedly blocked requests for a change in the operating strategy that required a consensus of 80% of the owning interests.

A project team had been put in place to update the serving reservoir model that had failed to predict the timing and extent of water breakthrough. I would be reporting to the Subsurface Manager, who was a Palestinian, by the name of Hafez H. Hafez. It's unknown whether his parents had gone for a triple with the middle initial, or only the double. His shaved bald head and features brought to mind Telly Savalas, the American character actor known as detective Kojak in the television crime series, whose tag line was, "Who Loves Ya Baby." Hafez was a humorless Kojak and that tag line was his as the project moved steadily toward failure, seemingly ending his career — the stress probably contributing to a sudden illness and his premature death, both occurring shortly after the end of my contract.

Why failure? Once again, just as in the prior projects for Maersk, Wintershall and BP, a geologist with supposedly little understanding of dynamic fluid flow became the de facto principal model architect. In this case, he was a young Indonesian contractor who reported to both Hafez and the Chief Geologist, managers who did not understand the modern, complex software used for model building by a new breed of geologist called a geo-modeler. When I learned that N_{res} / G arrays were not being used in the model building process, I requested a private meeting with the VP, there to explain the consequences of the planned modeling approach. He was told there would be a price to pay for building a model that would, in fact, be capable of predicting future reservoir performance. The price was a big one. It would mean supporting a reduction in booked oil reserves of 1-½ to 2 billion barrels, estimates based on 2 months of my evaluation using an interim test model. Prior models of Bu Hasa had been overly optimistic and the heart of the problem lay in the refusal to use N_{res} / G arrays. The senior executive was presented with a dilemma. If he called for following sound technical methodology, he would be calling for a cut in reserves. He really had no choice! It had been 42 years since I had first left Shell Oil Company, indignant that I had been asked to approve inflated reserve estimates for a California oil field, in retrospect a rare incident within Shell Oil Company. Now I accepted simply working as an adjunct to staff, doing as I was told. At least I had voiced my opinion.

A "Center of Excellence" was located on a separate floor of the ADCO building, staffed mostly by technical specialists from the SH companies. They kept a low profile, ostensibly overseeing technical matters on all of the onshore assets, including Bu Hasa. Why had they not foreseen the problems that led to the shut-in of 80,000 barrels per day of productive capacity? They probably had, but may have been reluctant to counter the views of ADCO. The Concession was set to expire in early 2014, after running its legal life of 75 years. Whether, or not, a SH would be awarded participation in a new Concession was determined solely by the Emirati owners. Why not hide and keep a low profile to avoid the risk of annoying the Master? The Chief Geologist was a representative of ExxonMobil and anything but quiet. He was a burly Bavarian who had tended bar while earning a PhD in geophysics from Clausthal University of Technology, one of the best in Germany. He looked like Theodore Roosevelt, with the same energy, hair, eyeglasses and swagger. Klaus Mueller (aka Teddy) was a tough, thick-skinned manager who, with a sense of humor, was popular with all groups of the UN Assembly that was ADCO. He seemingly knew little about reservoir simulation, which had matured as a technology while he was honing his natural leadership skills as a manager.

It was widely believed that the prolific carbonate reservoirs of Bu Hasa are naturally fractured. Fluids were expected to be flowing through open cracks in the rock in areas penetrated by the most productive wells. It was strange that a conceptual model was missing that might explain the observed high variation of well productivity. Natural fractures form in response to regional earth stresses, taking on a regular spacing and azimuth over large distances. Why were some areas at Bu Hasa highly productive and others only moderately productive? When the TS was in California, Kojak authorized payment for my weekend review of copious amounts of core descriptions, dating back over decades. The results were surprising. Natural fractures were frequently cited, but in nearly all cases they were filled with solid mineral material. They were not open! The common mention of vugs in the core descriptions raised awareness of a conceptual model that should have been the obvious first choice. As sea level cyclically fell and rose during geologic time, reef forming corals called *rudists* were repeatedly exposed to the atmosphere in a process called sub-aerial exposure. Given this depositional setting, meteoric water (rainfall) would have percolated through the coral shoals, thereby slowly dissolving the carbonate to form a connected mosaic of vugular pore space. This conceptual model is consistent with descriptions of the core material. High productivity wells would be expected when drilling into the ancient coral mounds, rather than into the mud-rich areas of low elevation that surround them. Images of the various rock types and their locations at Bu Hasa were available from seismic surveys, but they were not being used to build the reservoir model. If the seismic images were known to be incapable of revealing the presence of natural fractures, why use them?

The young geo-modeler had used only core data to build the reservoir model, delivered 9 months late for use in reservoir simulation. He had ignored the dynamic data from well tests and pressure transient analysis, repeating a key mistake made often, as had recently occurred in the Wintershall project in Russia. Flow capacity had been seriously underestimated in more than ½ of the wells, and the dynamic simulator was shown to be incapable of reproducing the historical reservoir performance. The project was stalled and the demands were tremendous to complete it, after many missed deadlines. Where was the missing flow capacity? Teddy and SH representatives from the Center of Excellence were provided with a summary of the core descriptions that did not support a naturally fractured reservoir model. At the same time, they were asked about the possible application of a sub-aerial exposure model — one that would support interconnected vugular pore space as the source of the missing flow capacity. The first response was that there had been no sub-aerial exposure!

Teddy then invited a local expert from the Petroleum Institute in Abu Dhabi for his views. Professor Thomas Steuber gave a talk at ADCO in which he strongly supported the sub-aerial exposure model, recommending mapping of the rudist shoals as a way forward. Once again, I sat listening to an academic, trying not to look smug. Not much time had passed since similar lessons had been taught to BP on the Wytch Farm field by an academic from the University of Aberdeen (Chapter 18). Hafez chose not to attend the presentation.

The Emiratis had been unknowable outside of the workplace. They live in palaces along the water or in high-walled compounds, each covering most of a city block. Only the glass in their vehicles could be tinted and only they could move freely, without queuing at airports or slowing with the flow of traffic. The country is run by guest workers, of both blue and white-collar denomination. It had been 18 months in Abu Dhabi when we returned home to California, punctuated only by a week's vacation in Greece.

CHAPTER TWENTY-ONE

TROUBLE WITH RUBBLE

The Kingdom of Bahrain is an archipelago of islands, the biggest of which is connected to Saudi Arabia by the King Fahd Causeway. Underlying most of that island is the Bahrain oil field, discovered in 1932. It has a big footprint, but its reservoirs are thin, holding only ~ 2-½% of Bu Hasa's oil in-place. One of the shallowest reservoirs contains heavy oil in a carbonate formation of low permeability, called the Mishrif (aka the Rubble), an accumulation that had not been tested using new thermal oil recovery methods. In 2009 with oil prices reaching 85 dollars per barrel, Occidental Petroleum Corp. (Oxy), Mubadala Development Co. (the sovereign wealth fund of the government of Abu Dhabi), and the National Oil & Gas Authority of Bahrain (NOGA) formed a joint operating company to further develop the Bahrain field, placing an emphasis on the Rubble. The joint entity and operator of the field was called Tatweer Petroleum. Stuart Walley had landed Mubadala as a new client. He secured my release from ADCO for several days, ostensibly to participate in a retreat being held for Senergy Associates. The retreat was actually going to be 3 days of meetings in Manama, the capital city of Bahrain, where the attendees would participate in what is called a Peer Review (or Peer Assist) of the Rubble field development plan (FDP) being proposed by Tatweer. I recall on the short flight from Abu Dhabi to Manama peering through partially open curtains into first class from my coach seat, there to view a small group of sheiks and American Special Ops military men traveling together. The contrast between the flowing white kanduras and keffiyehs of the Arabs and the camouflaged fatigues of the SO men was glaring, especially given the tattoos of snakes and daggers showing on the necks of the warriors. It brought to mind the planning of a clandestine operation that I, and generations of Americans to follow, would be paying for with tax dollars.

I registered at the Mercure Grand Hotel Seef, the venue chosen for the meetings, and went directly into its dining room for a late dinner. A group of men were openly discussing the project after finishing their meal, not knowing that a specialist from afar was in their midst. Their Texas accent was distinctive. They were undoubtedly the Oxy employees who had flown in from Houston. I had read the pre-meeting material and knew at once that I would not be able to support the proposed FDP. Tatweer were claiming that the Rubble reservoirs will perform like the diatomite reservoirs of California when subjected to cyclic steam injection. The two types of reservoirs have two main features in common: They are of low permeability and they contain heavy oil. I had learned a lot about reservoirs with these features through the two diatomite consortium research projects that I had initiated and directed as The Dietrich Corporation, 15 to 20 years earlier. Those projects had been co-funded by Arco, Mobil, Texaco and Unocal; Oxy had not joined that consortium. Results from the laboratory experimental program and the field pilot tests had not been shared with the industry, owing to confidentiality agreements that remained in effect. As an operator of heavy oil projects installed in conventional, high permeability, unconsolidated sand reservoirs in California and Oman, Oxy knew how to recover oil using steam. But they seemingly had little experience with the added test introduced by low permeability. I looked forward to the next several days. It would be good to mix with other men from the oil patch, many of them Americans. The challenge would be to gently push back on what was being proposed. There was no need to convince anyone of my views. Mubadala in Abu Dhabi was my client and they would be awaiting my recommendation on how to proceed.

The meetings opened on a Monday morning. There were 24 geoscientists and engineers in attendance: 10 from Tatweer, 11 from Oxy in Houston, Bakersfield (California) and Oman, 2 from Mubadala (including HS) and 1 from NOGA. I listened as several presenters from Tatweer described the plan: It involved piloting a cyclic steam process in two steps, first using 7 new wells and then quickly following with 55 additional wells. The pilot operations were expected to be followed by drilling more than 2,000 wells to eventually recover 160 million barrels of oil. It was dumbfounding that Oxy did not understand that the tight and thin Rubble did not contain a high enough concentration of oil to allow conventional thermal development. A well would need to heat an area of 7-½ to 10 acres of Rubble to produce enough oil for payout, an impossible order due to the high heat losses that would occur to the strata bounding the reservoir, a process made worse by the slow, conductive heating of the tight rock. Even in high permeability, heavy oil reservoirs, well spacing is typically limited to 1-¼ to 2-½ acres per well. The tight diatomite reservoirs are much thicker and wells drilled closely together — only tens of feet apart — routinely produce enough oil for payout. The key metric is the heavy oil in-place beneath an acre of surface area: Diatomite holds 250,000 to 350,000 barrels, whereas the Rubble holds only ~ 50,000 barrels.

How had Oxy missed the mark so widely? Their key project staff were from universities like Colorado School of Mines, Stanford and the University of Southern California, all known for having strong petroleum engineering programs. Perhaps it was because Oxy's strength lay in operating onshore oil fields, not in designing pilots for testing oil recovery technology — that was expertise provided by the majors like Chevron, ExxonMobil and Shell. Only one member of the Peer Assist team from Oxy was a reservoir engineer, a consultant from Houston who had recently retired from Shell, a man who apparently had little prior experience with tight oil reservoirs. All other Peer Assist members were geologists, or engineers expert in producing hot wells, or designing and operating the surface facilities needed for thermal oil recovery.

Upon my return to Abu Dhabi, I met with the VP of Development and the Chief Reservoir Engineer of Mubadala Petroleum, both Brits who had been hired from BP in Europe, a company with little, if any, experience in thermal oil recovery. I described why diatomite was not an analogue to the Rubble and proposed an alternative pilot design, one that would test application of the fracture assisted steamflood technology (called FAST), a technique patented by Conoco and pilot tested during the early 1980s in two tar sand reservoirs in Texas. The FAST results were encouraging. They were made public before the technology was shelved when oil prices fell steeply in 1986. Several more short trips to visit Tatweer were made during my contract with ADCO, each time consulting on behalf of Mubadala as a Senergy Associate.

When writing this chronicle I became curious about what had happened with the Rubble. That curiosity led to searching the Internet, where I learned that a technical paper had been presented at an industry conference in Muscat, Oman, in March 2016. Authored by several Tatweer employees, that paper described a series of failed pilot tests, starting with the very same pilot design that had been presented at the initial Peer Review meetings. None of the pilot projects tested the recommended FAST technology. Mubadala and Occidental Petroleum reached an agreement with the Bahrain government to exit Tatweer Petroleum, effective July 1, 2016.

CHAPTER TWENTY-TWO

LEGOS IN COPENHAGEN

It was early November, 2012. A staffing agency in London telephoned to learn of my interest in a contract position with Maersk Oil (MO) in Copenhagen. The caller and agency were unknown to me. They had seen my resume in what's now called *the cloud* that highlighted my prior contract with MO. Under that engagement, I had been directly hired by a Senior Vice President, who had left that company a few years later. That executive had been told by his staff that I was too independent to be considered for future contract work. I mentioned this during my telephone interview with a Development Director at MO, an American fresh on the job who was building a new project team. It was surprising that I was offered the contract, given my declaration that, indeed, I was not a team player. I would be reporting directly to the Development Director, a man who had jumped from one large company to another, most recently arriving from Hess Corporation in Malaysia, after residing and working in Nigeria with ExxonMobil. I sensed that he wanted a fellow American on the team that already consisted of members from Denmark, England, France, India, Italy and Norway.

The second entry into Copenhagen was difficult, unlike our initial entrance 7 years earlier, when MO had quickly secured a work permit on our behalf and paid our invoices by wiring funds directly into our American bank account. There had been no need to withhold taxes from our compensation. It had all been seamless, given the requirement that our stay in Denmark would be limited to a period of 6 months. That entry program for a citizen of a non-European Union country had been replaced by a complex, expensive and time consuming process. It started with downloading and completing an on-line application for a Danish residency and work permit that joined a letter of invitation sent on our behalf by MO to the Royal Norwegian Consulate General in San Francisco, where the Danes shared office space with the Norwegians. Once an application fee had been paid, I was given an appointment for a personal appearance at the Norwegian Consulate General's office, a requirement that meant air fare, hotel accommodation and meals for travel between Palm Springs and San Francisco. The good news was that the TS did not need to appear at the Consulate. Several weeks after the appointment, we flew to Copenhagen after receiving confirmation that all documents needed for issuance of the residency and work permit had been received there. It was not possible to begin the search for housing until we had opened a Danish bank account — that required obtaining something called a CPR number, which first required having our biometrics (facial scans and finger-prints) recorded at a difficult to find location in Copenhagen.

My contract was written with Spencer Ogden (SO), the staffing agency in London, for a duration of 18 months. They appointed IAT Base & Energy, a Danish entity, to act as agent on their behalf for administration of the contract, a service that included handling invoicing, payment and taxation matters. My invoices were sent monthly to SO in London. They included entries for my daily rate multiplied by the number of days worked, a housing allowance and authorized business-related travel expenses. SO in turn authorized IAT to pay the invoices, after withholding 26% of the gross amount for income tax and 8% of the gross for social services. An additional 3% of the gross was deducted by IAT for their handling fee. The top income tax rate in Denmark has averaged 61% over the last 20 years and it is now

56%. Of course in a Scandinavian welfare state like Denmark, these rates are normal. Why did I pay only 26% of the gross compensation as income tax? Under what's called the 48E taxation plan, a foreign worker is subject to a top income tax rate of 26% while working up to 5 years in Denmark, as a means of attracting highly skilled workers into the Danish work force. After 5 years, the worker can either shift to paying the normal welfare state tax rates, or leave the country. The majority of my expat colleagues chose to leave the country after 5 years rather than pay nearly 70% of their gross compensation for social services and income tax.

Upon arrival in Copenhagen, we registered at the Admiral Hotel, centrally located, on the waterfront, and only a 10-minute walk to the office. It was the hotel of choice 7 years earlier and not much had changed. There were little things about being in a European hotel again that were both enjoyable and annoying: The lack of sugar in the breakfast muesli was a good thing, whereas slow service at the bar was trying. If one is already paid a living wage as a bartender and tips are normally small, or missing altogether, as in most European countries, why hustle? After several weeks of Admiral living, the TS found a flat in Frederiksberg, an enclave of Copenhagen. It was located on a street called Gammel Kongevej (literally Old King's Road) in a neighborhood filled with shops, restaurants and pleasant parks, on the top floor of a 19th century building, reachable only by climbing 5 flights of stairs. The housing contract had been written with the estate agency that had shown the flat to the TS. After several months, the local landlord slipped a note under our door, politely mentioning that he had not received any rental payments. Our bank transfers had been received by the agency, but they had not paid our landlord. The agency had gone bankrupt! Our payments and the $10,000 security deposit paid by MO (that was to be held in escrow during the contract term) had vanished. The bankruptcy made front page news in the Copenhagen press, highly embarrassed the HR Department at MO and bilked the landlord out of two months rent. Notwithstanding this bad start, the flat and dealings with the landlord were to become the most agreeable of our expat encounters, once our bank transfers were made directly into his account.

The Development Director (DD) was anything but agreeable. He held a degree in earth science from the Colorado School of Mines and had worked in the Planning Departments of several major oil companies. He planned things, and that was about it. When a resume shows a series of movements from one large oil company to another and seemingly unpopular work locations like Malaysia and Nigeria, it's all telling: there's a problem with the potential for promotion of an individual. In this case, the problem was one of attitude and a lack of leadership skills, not intelligence. It seemed to me he was cheerless, a man without a sense of humor. At 5 feet, 7 inches in height, he did not seem to fit the adage, "Good things come in little packages."

When I received the interview call, the name Johan Sverdrup had been tagged to an oil field newly discovered in 2010, one that was undergoing appraisal drilling to understand its size and features. Taking the name of a 19th century distinguished prime minister of Norway, it's one of the biggest fields discovered in the North Sea. When it begins producing its designed, maximum plateau rate of 660,000 barrels of oil per day after 2019, it will be producing more oil than any other North Sea field, many of which are reaching their economic limit. Initially, ownership was shared among Statoil ASA (40%), Lundin (22.6%), Petoro (17.4%), Det Norske (11.6%) and Maersk Oil (8.4%). Statoil has been named operator of the venture, as a multi-national publicly owned oil company headquartered in Stavanger, with 67% of its stock owned by the Norwegian government. The early equity split was decided during July 2015 on the basis of a field development plan (FDP) prepared by Statoil and agreed by the 5 partners. MO could not simply accept estimates prepared by Statoil for the amount and distribution of oil at Johan Sverdrup, numbers that would later set the share of ownership. It was important for them to develop their own view of what lay beneath the various license areas, in preparation for future negotiations of equity share. And, of course, that involved building an in-house reservoir model of Johan Sverdrup, using shared data sourced from what would eventually become 31 newly drilled appraisal wells.

Two offices had been established: one in Copenhagen and one in Stavanger, Norway. There were a total of 22 subsurface team members, about equally split between the two locations, 18 of whom were company geologists, geophysicists and petrophysicists, professionals who live in a static world, intelligent and competent people who are trained to find oil accumulations, not to develop them. Only three team members and myself were reservoir engineers, specialists in the dynamics of fluid flow. The DD ceded control of reservoir modeling to a senior geologist, who became the principal model architect. He then set-up the team structure so that all reported to that person on matters related to modeling, except HS. My job was to understand the work of Statoil that was heavily based on reservoir simulation. Problems with their models were often the same as problems with MO's models. This meant that I could avoid directly critiquing what my team members were doing. They gradually became aware of their purported modeling shortcomings by listening to my presentations on the Statoil models.

It was actually Legos in Stavanger, not Legos in Copenhagen, where team building exercises were held using Legos, supposedly to improve cooperation between the two work locations. Legos are a product of Denmark. The Lego Group recently began marketing a consultancy service called *Lego Serious Play*, with the goal of fostering creative thinking in business. The methodology is described as, "A passionate and practical process for building confidence, commitment and insight." It all sounds like Danish hygge, group hugs and the pursuit of a cozy lifestyle.

MO had been operating Qatar's biggest offshore oil field — Al Shaheen — for nearly 25 years. While attending a peer review of operations at Al

Shaheen, I was shown an aerial view of horizontal wells that looked like a pile of pick-up sticks. It seemed they were not aware of mathematics that explained the benefits of drilling horizontal wells parallel to each other. That mistake had been made by Addax Petroleum in Geneva, where the diverse trajectories of the horizontal development wells had been decided by geologists, people who were seemingly unknowing about the dynamics of fluid flow. Uncontrollable breakthrough of injected gas to the "pile of sticks" in the Addax reservoirs had led to disappointing performance and may have contributed to the early sale of that privately owned company to the China Petrochemical Corporation (Sinopec).

The Lego retreat was held during the year 2013, when the Brent oil price was more than $100 per barrel. They have recently lost the contract to operate Al Shaheen, thereby losing up to 40% of their total productive capacity. Weakened by that unexpected event and much lower oil prices, MO became too small to be listed as a stand-alone company. They sold all of their assets to Total S.A. in early 2018.

CHAPTER TWENTY-THREE

MAGICAL MADRID

There was to be one more contract before the business phone would no longer ring. That final project was preceded by several false starts. The first was a contract offer received from Dong Energy in Copenhagen, with Spencer Ogden from London again acting as the broker. There were several issues that prevented working for Dong, an operator of oil fields in the Danish North Sea and the biggest provider of wind energy in Europe: First, the housing market had tightened and it was no longer possible to sign a housing contract as a citizen of a non-European country without sponsorship from a Danish company — support that was not forthcoming; secondly, it would not have been possible to work in the normal manner as The Dietrich Corporation, meaning that a significant portion of gross income could not have been sheltered from taxation by placing it into our corporate 401k plan; and finally, Dong was unwilling to pay temporary hotel living costs while we were house-hunting in Copenhagen — the risks were high that we would be stuck in expensive hotel living. It was primarily the intransigence of Dong and the feeling that we were not welcome that caused me to void the contract the night before my fly date.

The second contract offer was received from RusPetro Plc, a small operator located in Moscow and publicly traded on the UK stock exchange. It was rumored that company was close to bankruptcy, notwithstanding efforts of the Don and Joe Show, an act that had resurfaced at RusPetro Plc following the demise of Yukos. And finally, in what will probably mark the last business opportunity based on my network of connections, the Dubai office of an energy consultancy expressed interest in my employment. Their Manager of Reservoir Engineering had a favorable recall of Todd, Dietrich & Chase, Inc., a company that had been closed for 25 years! I passed on both closeness to bankruptcy and employment, remembering that it was contract work, even while serving as an adjunct to staff, that allowed the most autonomy. Given these disappointing opportunities and feeling the need for international travel, we planned a personal trip to Spain, where we had not previously lived as expats. That 2-½ week road trip was to put a cap on our global escapades.

That was until Senergy Resources Ltd. called a few weeks after we had returned home, offering a contract in Madrid with Compania Espanola de Petroleos, S.A.U. (CEPSA). What a coincidence! The sovereign wealth fund of Abu Dhabi had recently bought CEPSA and the Abu Dhabi National Oil Company (ADNOC) wanted to evaluate the technical expertise of the Spanish staff. What better way to do this than by having them prepare a series of field development plans (FDPs) for Abu Dhabi reservoirs in competition with another company. The Abu Dhabi government and Japan were close to signing a contract that would fix a long-term supply of petroleum products to Japan — ADNOC chose Inpex, Japan's biggest oil and gas E&P company to prepare the comparative FDPs on the same series of Abu Dhabi reservoirs.

I was recruited for the job by a man serving as the CEPSA technical manager of the project and known to me from my prior Senergy contract in Abu Dhabi. A suitable contract was cut between Senergy and The Dietrich Corporation, one that provided for reimbursement of hotel living costs and a daily per-diem. Senergy wanted to make a reservation for me at the Hotel Eurostars, a 4-star luxury accommodation adjacent to CEPSA's offices in the suburbs of Madrid, where the entire team was staying. I knew that would not work for me or the TS, what with modern high-rise architecture, box-like rooms with inoperable windows, and a remoteness from all that was happening after business hours in the center of Madrid. The housing issue became quite contentious, with Senergy yielding control only when I refused to sign the contract without having the freedom to choose my own housing. We chose the boutique Hotel Petit Palace Lealtad Plaza, located in central Madrid adjacent to Parque del Retiro and within 2 blocks of the Prado Museum. It was to be a perfect location, where my colleagues joined us on occasional evenings to escape their austere, remotely located lodgings.

The team met for introductions in the bar of the Hotel Eurostars after the first day of work. In attendance were the technical manager of the project and his son, a recent petroleum engineering graduate of Heriot Watt University in Edinburgh, and 4 Senergy consultants, including 3 earth scientists and myself. During casual conversation, the manager recalled for the group that the project was to proceed in 2 phases. Phase 1 had been awarded to Senergy; it was to be a major review and quality check of the available data. Phase 2 had not yet been awarded; it was to involve design of the FDPs using reservoir simulation. I wondered why the manager was retelling what was already known. All became clear when he openly stated that Phase 2 would also likely be awarded to Senergy, given two conditions: the first was a demonstrated good performance in Phase 1; the second was an employment contract for his son! The Regional Manager for Senergy smoothly handled the blatant quid-pro-quo, buying time without skipping a beat, or spilling his glass of Rioja wine. It was as though he had expected the backhander, notwithstanding the public nature of its expression.

The focus of the project was on 3 small carbonate reservoirs onshore in the Emirate of Abu Dhabi, with names Mirfa, Ruwais and South Huwaila, where the oil is held in the same strata as at Bu Hasa — in a system of interconnected vugs, or small caverns, that have formed via sub-aerial exposure and leaching due to percolating rainwater. The project manager for Senergy was a geologist with a PhD from Imperial College London. He was from Iran, home of the Asmari oil fields, prime examples of anticlinal traps and the effects of structurally controlled fracturing on reservoir performance. The subject of his PhD dissertation had been reservoir fracture identification, prediction, characterization and modeling in carbonate and clastic reservoirs. Although he had been the head of a so-called Fracture Team at Senergy for a decade, he had little specific experience with the rocks of the subject reservoirs. I wondered if this de-facto model architect had a fracture fetish, whereby, in his world, there was no possibility of fluid flow through interconnected vugular pore space in the carbonates of the UAE He refused to review files of core descriptions from Bu Hasa, all of which described the common occurrence of vugs. When fractures were reported for that analogue reservoir, they were always described as being filled with natural cements — they were closed due to mineralization. He seemed as closed as the fractures themselves — incapable of reviewing the data and considering an alternative model. It was galling to listen to his admittedly excellent presentation of how fractures form in response to regional stresses, practiced after many deliveries to many audiences, never mind that fractures were not expected to be relevant for development of the subject reservoirs. It was all like teaching the Theory of Isostasy instead of Plate Tectonics.

One may ask, "Does it make any difference whether fluid flows through fractures or interconnected vugs"? The answer is yes. Wells, to be highly productive, need to penetrate either fractured regions of the reservoir, or regions containing lots of vugs. Wells would be drilled and completed in different locations depending on the conceptual model of the reservoir. Given the nature of the reservoir model in a possible Phase 2 that would be carried-out in Abu Dhabi, I gave notice to Senergy that I would not be available after Phase 1.

Two years after leaving Madrid, bilateral agreements between Japan and the UAE have strengthened, especially in the areas of energy and exploration of space. Japanese banks have recently loaned the UAE several billion dollars, in efforts to help Japanese companies renew oilfield concessions, 60% of which are set to expire in 2018. Senergy Resources Ltd. was indeed awarded Phase 2 of the contract and the son of the project manager was later employed by them in Aberdeen, Scotland, most likely as a very competent and grateful young engineer. Unknown at the time, the Madrid contract was to be my last. Oil prices have retreated to record sustained lows, in a downturn that is the deepest in the 50 years of my career. It may have been fate that led me to choose a hotel in the center of Madrid, immediately adjacent to the beautiful Parque del Retiro, a Spanish name that sounds like Park of the Retired and actually translates to Park of the Retreat.

Part Three

Write-Down
of Reserves

CHAPTER TWENTY-FOUR

MOONBEAM MODELING

As a young politician, former Governor Jerry Brown of California proposed some novel ideas — two involved establishing a state space academy and placing a satellite into orbit for the purpose of providing emergency communications services. He was given the nickname *Moonbeam* by a Chicago Sun-Times columnist, Mike Royko, as a result of his shared creative thinking, a sobriquet that quickly became synonymous with the words idealistic, impractical and optimistic. Royko publicly expressed regret for tagging Brown with a moniker that became difficult to shake, especially when more than a few of the politician's fresh proposals were eventually taken seriously and adopted. In the end, the word *moonbeam* left pixie dust, not dirt. There was humor in it — its usage was benign, causing no real damage. Not so as used here, where the words *Moonbeam Modeling* are used to describe an overly optimistic reservoir modeling process that underlies what has become a systematic overstatement of hydrocarbon reserves.

Central to understanding the recent trend of reserves overbooking is the subject matter of Production Attainment (PA). PA is the ratio of actual production to the production promised at project sanction, an assurance often based on reservoir modeling. As first revealed in 2010 by a series of project look-backs and petroleum industry surveys, PA was found to be worsening over a 15-year period. Projects starting in 1995 were delivering on average a PA of 94%, whereas projects starting in 2010 were delivering on average a PA of only 75%! It was alarming to read an introductory paper on this topic, listing so-called root causes for deficient production. Upon becoming more familiar with the subject, it was puzzling why the petroleum industry did not jump on the revealed findings with vigor, moving with determination to improve the situation. Making known that overly optimistic reservoir description is a major part of the problem was in itself a really good start. But simply defining root causes of deficiency as, "Assumed continuous sand sheet model; turns out not to be the case," or "Major reduction in plateau rate due to lower than assumed recovery factor," leaves open the question of what fundamentally is going awry with reservoir modeling.

The revealed fall in production attainment is equivalent to an inflation of what are called PDP (proved, developed and producing) reserves. That this eye-opener relates to the PDP reserves category is especially troubling — PDP reserves are expected to be the most reliably predictable! The value of a hydrocarbon-bearing asset is basically set by the sum of its PDP and PUD (proved, undeveloped) reserves. When learning of this news in 2014, it occurred that several of the so-called root causes of overly optimistic reservoir description could be linked to the industry's move away from the time-honored use of N_{res} / G property arrays (Chapter 25). This particular shift in the reservoir modeling process has been the bane of my technical life, and that of many other reservoir engineers. It has prompted me to leave several contracts early, when the client insisted on ignoring established procedures that had been used for decades to estimate recoverable reserves. The procedural shift took place in the mid-1990s, a period that saw the introduction of powerful earth modeling software and a major transfer in control of reservoir simulation technology from the reservoir engineering to the earth science disciplines. Prior to this, it had rarely been necessary to write down reserves, as a means of complying with U.S. Security and Exchange

Commission rules. More recently, during the increasing dominion of earth science, reserve write-downs have become commonplace. Early, encouraging findings based on audits of U.S. reserves estimates showed that, "Most of the reserves estimates submitted to the Energy Information Agency between 1977 and 1997 are more than 90% certain to be recovered, and, in many cases, are more than 95% certain to be recovered." In contrast, between 2003 and 2008, E&P companies reported negative revisions of more than 9.3 billion net BOE* (equivalent oil barrels) of proved reserves, including huge write-downs by the Royal Dutch Shell Group, El Paso Corporation, Stone Energy Corporation, Repsol YPF and more than a dozen other publicly traded companies. And all this during a period of rising oil prices!

---

*A unit of energy based on the approximate energy released by burning one barrel (42 U.S. gallons) of crude oil. The BOE is used by oil and gas companies in their financial statements as a way of combining oil and natural gas reserves and production into a single measure.

CHAPTER TWENTY-FIVE

THE BIG SHIFT

The topic of N/G ratio is highly polarizing. It divides many within the petroleum industry, most often earth scientists and engineers. Discussion of it is likened to debate of politics or religion. Simply put, the obsession among engineers with using N_{res} / G ratio arrays stems from their need for modeling variations in the connectivity of the holes in the rock that contain oil, water and gas. Better connectivity means better oil recovery, which in turn means greater company value. It's all about the dynamics for the engineer! The earth scientist is focused on the ultimate (original) resource in-place. It's all about the statics for him! He often misses the point that value is assigned to recoverable reserves, not to total hydrocarbon volumes held in the earth.

When a client refused to use N_{res} / G arrays, I left projects early, each time per a contract clause that allowed either party to terminate without penalty given at least 30-days notice. That happened four times. The first early exit led to a short break, occurring at the beginning of a project for Deminex in 1996. Powerful earth modeling computer codes were just becoming commercially available at that time, marking a shift in control of reservoir model building from the reservoir engineering to the earth science disciplines. A product called IRAP-RMS™ was the first on the market, developed by the Norwegian group Smedvig Technologies AS and appearing in 1995. It had been licensed by the earth science group at Deminex in Essen, who upon my arrival said "Surprise! This project marks a new dawn. You will be reporting to a young geologist who has just completed an introductory IRAP-RMS™ training course." Bleary-eyed, heavy with jet-lag and learning that Ivan the Wonderful (Chapter 7) was on vacation and unable to ensure my normal protected status, I quickly returned to California, cooling my heels while a power struggle played out in the client company. A week later I returned to Germany upon learning that once again I would be serving as the principal model architect, reporting to Ivan as the Director of Engineering. That was my last major modeling project controlled by an engineer. The year was 1996. It was indeed a new dawn! Reservoir modeling had become the dominion of earth science.

The second, third and fourth walk-outs occurred later while working for Chevron in Bangkok (Chapter 15), Wintershall in Moscow (Chapter 16) and Maersk in Copenhagen (Chapter 22). In each case, at least a year had passed before moving on. When not leading to an early exit, saying, "No," to the use of N_{res} / G arrays often led to acrimony, as happened again at Maersk (Chapter 14), BP in Aberdeen (Chapter 18) and ADCO in Abu Dhabi (Chapter 20).

It was surprising that an individual company did not have a consistent view on this important subject. How strange, given that reservoir modeling is the workhorse of field development planning and production forecasting! The office of ExxonMobil in Hanover, Germany, had embraced the use of N_{res} / G arrays on their Soehlingen gas reservoirs, whereas the ExxonMobil Chief Geologist in Abu Dhabi had refused their use on Bu Hasa. And then the North Sea Headquarters of BP in Aberdeen had agreed to use N_{res} / G arrays on Wytch Farm only after lengthy debate and my provision of written confirmation that a highly competent consulting group (International Reservoir Technologies, Inc.) had been (and was still) using them on Prudhoe Bay in Alaska, the second crown jewel of BP. Why the inconsistency? The answer may relate to the oddly different messages seemingly endorsed by the Society of Petroleum Engineers (SPE) and the American Association of

Petroleum Geologists (AAPG), an earth scientist's professional organization of choice.

The SPE supports an approach to model building that eliminates hydrocarbons initially in-place in rock of relatively poor quality, where little or no flow is expected to occur. In fact, it publishes guidelines that explicitly call for the use of N_{res} / G arrays:

> "Typically, information on regional and local geology are (is) used to construct net-to-gross (NTG) maps (obtained from the nearby analogue reservoirs after applying parameter cutoffs to exclude portions of the reservoir that do not meet the minimum criteria to support production), and integrated with gross reservoir volume to yield net pay maps,"

and Board Members of the AAPG explicitly sanction the SPE guidelines. This endorsement notwithstanding, a different slant is promoted by on-line websites of earth scientists — one in which models are built using estimates of total hydrocarbons in-place. The AAPG WIKI website states that OOIP and OGIP "refer to the total volume of hydrocarbon stored in a reservoir prior to production." The E&P Geology website is a "free on-line community that aims to bring petroleum professionals and geologists together and share valuable knowledge." The following is a quotation from their website:

> "N/G cutoffs seem to come from an era when hydrocarbon accumulations were mainly calculated through map-based techniques either on paper or on simple workstations. With 3D reservoir modeling, the need for making a specific N/G property to cut out bad porosity and low HC saturation seems a little unnecessary. The low porosity and low HC-saturation cells simply add little extra hydrocarbon volume."

These websites have had tens of thousands of "hits" — it's disappointing that confusion is introduced in this manner. It's an important topic — an overly optimistic view of recovery factor results when reservoir models for dynamic simulation are built using the total hydrocarbon methodology. When this occurs, estimates of ultimate recovery factor will seldom be achievable due to an inability to produce noncontributing hydrocarbon volumes stored in non-reservoir rock. The difference between what's called Net Reservoir and Net Rock is at the heart of the matter.

The term Net Reservoir Volume (N_{res}) has been used by reservoir and petroleum engineers for decades. Its use in reservoir modeling allows recovery efficiency to be evaluated meaningfully by dividing producible hydrocarbons by an initial volume of hydrocarbons held in rock that is capable of flowing reservoir fluids.

A different approach to model building began during the dominion of earth science, starting in the mid-1990s and replacing the routine, earlier use of Net Reservoir Volume. The term Net Rock Volume (N_{rock}) was introduced to describe the proportion of the Gross Rock Volume (GRV) that is capable of storing hydrocarbons, without regard to the potential for fluid flow. Net Rock Volume includes all hydrocarbon-stained rock. It holds the highest estimate of hydrocarbons in-place, one that stores a portion of the total volume that will neither move nor support reservoir pressure, regardless of the applied recovery process.

There's a wide variation of the proportion of total hydrocarbon volume that will not flow, varying from nearly "0" for most parts of really great reservoirs — like those of Johan Sverdrup (Chapter 22) — to nearly "1" for many parts of really poor reservoirs — like those of Novy Urengoy (Chapter 16). A number of "1/3" is a reasonable single low estimate for application worldwide, implying that only "2/3", or less, of so-called proved reserves are movable. In other words, proved reserves on average are *Too Much by Half*.

EPILOGUE

The trend of omitting a N_{res} / G ratio array during reservoir model building invariably results in an overstatement of reserves and asset value. Is this being done purposely, with good-old greed as the driving force? If not, what are the other underlying human factors that may be at play? Ignorance, the need to please, a lack of leadership, and apathy are all possible answers to this question. All these factors contribute to the problem, but apathy and ignorance take top billing.

Why highlight apathy? It was a discerning writer who penned "Reserve Overbooking — The Problem No One Wants to Talk About." Reserve overbooking (or a deficiency of production attainment) is indeed the elephant in the room! In 2015 following my final consulting services contract, I applied to be a Society of Petroleum Engineers Distinguished Lecturer for the 2016-2017 year. My topic was, "Bridging the Modeling Divide Between Earth Science and Engineering," the heart of which described reservoir modeling practices that ostensibly underlie the deficiency of production attainment. The topic was not selected by the Distinguished Lecturer Committee. Disappointed but determined to share my experience with others, I tried a different approach in 2016. That was a mass mailing to 100 colleagues in Big Oil and academia, proposing an on-campus training course entitled "The Production Attainment Initiative," the net profits of which would be shared with sponsoring academic Departments of Petroleum Engineering. The proposal was carefully prepared and packaged in a professional manner, forwarded via the U.S. Postal Service, both globally and domestically. It was a custom, old-school style of marketing, from one technical person to another, raising the issue that I had found so troubling upon its discovery. The response? Two highly distinguished colleagues replied via the Internet: Tom Blasingame from Texas A&M University was on sabbatical and unavailable to consider the proposition; Khalid Aziz of Stanford University was highly encouraging and recommended continuing with the effort. Other response? Zero — absolute silence from 98 of 100 recipients of the proposal. There was total indifference, or apathy!

And why emphasize ignorance? It's because when production attainment started falling about 20 years ago, there was a widespread push to decentralize and flatten organizations, a drive that resulted in reservoir simulation being performed locally rather than by centralized groups of specialists. Local staff are focused on daily operations and business cycle activity — they have no time to become specialists in complex technology that requires long periods of unbroken concentration for proficiency. If their interests lay in reservoir modeling, they would have pursued PhD degrees and chosen consulting, research or academia for a career, not life in the fast-moving, exciting pace of an operating company. In an article published in 1997 entitled "Reservoir Simulation: Past, Present and Future," it was considered that 20-years in the future (i.e. in the year 2017), "A critical issue will be integration of reservoir simulation with earth modeling." How prophetic! Furthermore, it was stated that, "Management believes R&D related to reservoir simulation should compress calendar time, decrease costs and reduce expertise required." Something seems amiss with a call to reduce the expertise required for reservoir modeling, right? Yet there is no reason to think that the author conveyed the wrong message. He was a consummate professional, a Research Advisor with Exxon Production Research Company, specializing in the development of computational techniques for use in reservoir simulation and a member of the *SPE Journal Editorial Board*. What was the business driver behind the call by management to decentralize reservoir modeling and place it in the hands of non-specialists? Arguably, it may have been the need of the hardware and software industry in 1997 to monetize reservoir modeling to the fullest — to have it become a billion dollar space in the 21st century. Powerful PCs sitting globally on a sea of desktops, either standing alone, or accessing a network of servers, running multiple software licenses and requiring annual fees for upgrades and maintenance, were the dream of the future — one that has come true.

Decentralization of reservoir modeling is not only good for those who manufacture computers and develop simulation software — it underlies the changes that took place in the style of contract employment. Until 1997, consulting reservoir engineers were free to market their services and control the technical aspects of a client study. Then that style changed quickly (Chapter 8). Staffing agencies were born. Contractors were placed on-site, working as adjuncts to staff, rapidly replaceable given reluctance to take direction from the client, direction that often encouraged overstatement of reserves. Opportunities for working as an independent consultant fell rapidly in number.

Misguided incentives and competition for investors are factors that are neither technical nor human in nature. Yet they too bring about overly optimistic reservoir description and deficiency of production attainment. The Iran-Conoco-Affair was born out of a competition for investors (Chapter 4). That scandal had nothing to do with production promised at project sanction (or approval). It had to do with a corporation avoiding injunctions (sanctions — in a different sense of the word) placed on Iran by the U.S. State Department. The misguided incentive was the promise of campaign finance contributions in return for laissez-faire enforcement of existing sanctions laws. The U.S. Department of Energy (DOE) was one of the few federal agencies not involved in the Iran-Conoco affair. It has its own style of providing misguided incentives, one that is not as blatant as a simple quid-pro-quo. When it subsidizes commercialization of technology by distributing public money for demonstration of activities such as reservoir characterization and carbon capture and sequestration (CCS), the recipients of public funding must downplay less than positive results, or risk losing their contracts.

There's a parallel between Wall Street and the evolved style of doing business as an adjunct to staff. Mathematical models are fundamental to the worlds of finance and oil. Those who develop them are called quants in the financial world and developers in the oil world. The models are used to establish value and risk. Credit ratings and values of companies in each world are evaluated and supposedly made transparent to potential investors by regulators and ratings agencies. But the real commonality is that few in leadership positions understand what's inside the models (i.e. simulators), or their limitations. It's implied that at Morgan Stanley, neither John Mack as CEO nor one Howie Hubler, as head of the bond-trading desk, was capable of understanding that bond firm's trading risks. And Chuck Prince, the former CEO of Citigroup, was reportedly trained as a lawyer, not a quant; it's said he delegated responsibility for understanding the risks of new and complex financial instruments (the so-called derivatives) to others. That's understandable — how could anyone other than a quant understand something called VaR, or statistical Gaussian copula techniques used for modeling risk? And how could anyone other than a developer, or specialist in simulating the dynamics of fluid flow, understand the effects of numerical dispersion, heavy-end dropout, or something called surface film drainage?

Moonbeam Modeling and its flaws have led to a fall in production attainment and inflation of oil reserves — we're likely moving faster than thought toward the end of the oil age. In a similar way, flaws in the financial models of Wall Street have led to a melt down of the global financial system — and they may again. Financiers pretend that economics is science, playing as if they are STEM people. *Moonbeam* geologists *are real scientists*. Their over-optimism is requisite for finding natural resources. They mean well, unlike the financiers who dreamt-up derivatives out of greed and unleashed a global catastrophe. I'll take moonbeams and pixie dust any day.

NOTES

PREFACE

He tells us we're at the dawn of the fossil fuel era: see Tracy, Rex, *The Dawn of the Fossil Fuel Era: The End of "Peak Oil"*, Amazon, 2016.

The debate on peak oil was over, and the peakists have won: see Auzanneau, Matthieu, *Oil Power and War - A Dark History*, Chelsea Green, 2018, p. 519.

90% of American shale operators had a negative cash flow: see Auzanneau, Matthieu, *Oil Power and War - A Dark History*, Chelsea Green, 2018, p. 548.

"Shale oil in the ground is not oil at all - it was so named in order to attract investment": see Goodstein, David, *Out of Gas*, Norton, 2004, pp. 31-32.

The ratio is about 40 years for oil and 60 years for natural gas: see Goodstein, David, *Out of Gas*, Norton, 2004, p. 120.

CHAPTER TWO

We published its results in a technical paper: Dietrich, J.K. and Little, J.E., *A Method for Determining Reservoir Fluid Saturations Using Field Production Data*, *SPE J*. 15 (6), 1975, pp. 477-486.

The lifted knowledge had its roots in research: Dougherty. E. https:// ethw.org/ *First-Hand:The_Evolution_of_the_ARAMCO_ Reservoir_ Behavior _ Simulator_ (ARBS)*, 2015.

The first major reservoir simulation project in Shell: Dietrich, J.K., *Recognition of Acceleration and Additional Oil Recovery Opportunities Using Numerical Reservoir Simulation Techniques,* https://doi.org/10.2118/4601-MS, 1973.

CHAPTER THREE

Standard for the design and evaluation of CO$_2$ injection: Chase, C.A. Jr. and Todd, M.R., *Numerical Simulation of CO$_2$ Flood Performance, SPE J.* 24 (6), 1984, pp. 597-605.

We demonstrated with thermal reservoir simulation: Dietrich, J.K., *Steamflooding in a Water Drive Reservoir, Upper Tulare Sands – South Belridge Field, SPE Res Eng* 5 (3), 1990, pp. 275-284.

Industry was aware that these same discontinuous lenses: Neuman, C.H. *A Mathematical Model of the Steam Drive Process Applications,* https://doi. org/10.2118/4757-MS, 1975.

The already published effect of overlapping shale: Prats, M., *The Influence of Oriented Arrays of Thin Impermeable Shale Lenses or of Highly Conductive Natural Fractures on Apparent Permeability Anisotropy. J Pet Technol* 24 (10), 1972, pp. 1219-1221.

Pilot project produced at sluggish rates predicted by the simulator: Dietrich, J.K., *The Kern River Horizontal Well Steam Pilot, SPE Res Eng* 3 (3), 1988, pp. 935-944.

His paper published years earlier on oil well casing stresses: Willhite, G.P. and Dietrich, W.K., *Design Criteria for Completion of Steam Injection Wells, J Pet Technol* 19 (01), https://doi.org/10.2118/1560-PA, 1967, pp. 15-21.

CHAPTER FOUR

More than 100 wells had been lost in the South Belridge field alone: Fast, R.E., Murer, A.S. and Zambrano, L.G., *Lost Hills Diatomite Simulation Study: Predicting Waterflood Performance in a Low-Permeability, Compacting Reservoir*, https://doi.org/10.2118/26627-MS, 1993.

Breaking wellbores were hugely expensive and a common problem: De Rouffignac, E.P., Bondor, P.L., Karanikas, J.M., and Hara, S.K., *Subsidence and Well Failure in the South Belridge Diatomite Field*, https://doi.org/10.2118/29626-MS, 1995.

Concern there had been to prevent the Orinoco River from overflowing: Chase, C.A. Jr. and Dietrich, J.K., *Compaction Within the South Belridge Diatomite, SPE Res Eng* 4 (4), https://doi.org/10.2118/17415-PA, 1989, pp. 422-428.

Described what happened in an article entitled, "The Iran-Conoco Affair": Parsons, R.K. *The Iran-Conoco Affair*. http://iran-conoco-affair.us, 2000.

CHAPTER SEVEN

There is a basic assumption in geostatistics: Hewett, T.A. and Behrens, R.A., *Conditional Simulation of Reservoir Heterogeneity With Fractals, SPE Form Eval* 5 (3), https://doi.org/10.2118/18326-PA, 1990, pp. 422-428.

In that key publication on pinnacle reef reservoirs: Mungan, N., Nelson, D.J., and Lee Wing, B.M, *Enhanced Oil Recovery Possibilities for Pembina Nisku C-Pool*, https://doi.org /10.2118/8383-MS , 1979.

CHAPTER NINE

A process called surface film drainage: Salathiel, R.M, *Oil Recovery by Surface Film Drainage in Mixed-Wettability Rocks, J Pet Technol* 25 (10), https://doi.org/10.2118/4104-PA, 1973, pp. 1216-1224.

CHAPTER TWELVE

Designing a company petroleum engineering training program in Moscow: Wolcott, D., *A Recent History of the Russian Oil Industry and a Look to Its Future*, World Energy, 7 (3), 2004, pp. 139-144.

Economides claimed that the maximum achievable J_D is $6/\pi$: Oligney, R.E., Valko, P. and Economides, M.J, see *Unified Fracture Design — Bridging the Gap Between Theory and Practice*, Orsa Press, 2001.

They had just prepared and submitted two manuscripts for presentation: see Demarchos, A.S., Chomatas, A.S., Economides, M.J. et al., *Pushing the Limits in Hydraulic Fracture Design*, https://doi.org/10.2118/86483-MS, 2004; and Economides, M.J., Demarchos, A.S., Mach, J.M. et al., *Pushing the Limits of Hydraulic Fracturing in Russia*, https://doi.org/10.2118/90357-MS, 2004.

Presenting my results on J_D as if they were their own: Rueda, J.I., Mach, M. and Wolcott, D., *Pushing Fracturing Limits to Maximize Producibility in Turbidite Reservoirs in Russia*, https://doi.org/10.2118/ 91760-MS, 2004.

Presented $4/\pi$ and all that it meant as if there had never been a question: see Sabaev, V.V., Mach, J.M., Wolcott, D.S. et al., *Vertically Fractured Well Performance in Rectangular Drainage Area*, https://doi.org/ 10.2118/101048-MS, 2006.

Surprising that my work had not been referenced: Dietrich, J.K., *J_D As A Performance Indicator for Hydraulically Fractured Wells*, https://doi.org/10.2118/93630-MS, 2005.

They resurfaced after the demise of Yukos: Helmer, J., *RusPetro — The Little Oil Well That Waters a Billion Dollar Dream*. Posted in Oil & Gas, UK-Russia, 28 April, article printed from *Dances With Bears*: http://johnhelmer.net, 2012.

CHAPTER SEVENTEEN

Benefits of drilling horizontal wells parallel to each other: see Suprunowicz, R. and Butler, R.M., *The Choice of Pattern Size and Shape for Regular Arrays of Horizontal Wells, J Can Pet Technol* 31 (1), https://doi.org/10.2118/92-01-04, 1992, pp. 39-44.

Only the bitumen and heavy oil occurring within the least heterogeneous: Dietrich, J.K., *Shale Lenses Limit Commercial Application of SAGD Process, Oil & Gas J.* 110 (12), 2012, pp. 92-99.

CHAPTER EIGHTEEN

Modeling philosophy called Top Down Reservoir Modeling: Williams, G.J.J., Mansfield, M. and MacDonald, D.G. et al., *Top-Down Reservoir Modeling*, https://doi.org/10.2118/89974-MS, 2004.

Talk that discredited interpretations of the geology long held by BP and TRACS: North, C.P. and Davidson, S.K, *Wytch Farm – BP – Review of Lithofacies and Environmental Interpretations*, Power Point Presentation, AUDRI Rivers and Related Sediments, University of Aberdeen, Kings College, 2009.

CHAPTER TWENTY-ONE

That paper described a series of failed pilot tests: Al Balushi, A., Mohamed, A. and Stearns, S., *The Chronology of Steam Piloting in the Rubble Heavy Oil Reservoir, Awali Field, Bahrain*, https://doi.org/10.2118/ 179846-MS, 2016.

CHAPTER TWENTY-FOUR

Central to understanding the recent trend of reserves overbooking is the subject matter of Production Attainment (PA): Nandurdikar, N.S. and Wallace, L., *Failure to Produce, An Investigation of Deficiencies in Production Attainment*, https://doi.org/10.2118/ 145437-MS, 2011.

Reported negative revisions of more than 9.3 billion net BOE (equivalent oil barrels) of proved reserves: Olsen, G.T., Lee, W.J. and Blasingame, T.A., *Reserves Overbooking: The Problem We're Finally Going To Talk About*, https://doi.org/10.2118/134014-MS, 2010.

CHAPTER TWENTY-FIVE

It publishes guidelines that explicitly call for the use of N_{res} / G arrays: Society of Petroleum Engineers, *Guidelines for Application of the Petroleum Resources Management System, Section 4.2.2 Volumetric and Analogous Methods*, 2011.

AAPG WIKI website states that OOIP and OGIP refer to the total: AAPG WIKI. *Development Geology Reference Manual, Reservoir Engineering Methods, Reserves Estimation* http://wiki.aapg.org/Reserves_estimation, February, 2016.

Need for making a specific N/G property to cut out bad porosity and low HC saturation seems a little unnecessary: Exploration & Production Geology, *Production Geology, General Discussion, NTG or N/G: Defining Net Cut Offs*, http://www.epgeology.com, November, 2014.

EPILOGUE

Reserve overbooking (or a deficiency of production attainment) is indeed the elephant in the room: McLane, M.A. and Rose, P.R., *Reserve Overbooking — The Problem No One Wants to Talk About*, https://doi.org/10.2118/68580-MS, 2001.

A critical issue will be integration of reservoir simulation with earth modeling: Watts, J.W., *Reservoir Simulation: Past, Present and Future*, SPE Computer Applications, *SPE J.* 9 (6), https://doi.org/ 10.2118/38441-PA, 1997, pp. 171-176.

Head of the bond-trading desk, was capable of understanding that bond firm's trading risks: see Lewis, M., *The Big Short,* London, England, Penguin Books, Ltd., 2010, pp. 217-218

Delegated responsibility for understanding the risks of new and complex financial instruments (the so-called derivatives) to others: Tett, G., *Fool's Gold,* London, England, Little, Brown Book Group, 2009, p. 160.

GLOSSARY

BOE (barrel of oil equivalent)
A unit of energy based on the approximate energy released by burning one barrel (42 U.S. gallons) of crude oil. The BOE is used by oil and gas companies in their financial statements as a way of combining oil and natural gas reserves and production into a single measure, although this energy equivalence does not take into account the lower financial value of energy in the form of gas.

BSCM (billions of standard cubic meters)
Units commonly applied for the volume of gas or gas condensate production or reserves.

DOE (U.S. Department of Energy)
Specifically the Office of Fossil Energy.

EOR (enhanced oil recovery)
A term used for a number of recovery processes applied to recover oil that may not be producible by natural pressure depletion or water injection. The injection of heat, polymer, surfactants and carbon dioxide are all examples of EOR processes.

FDP (field development plan)

A plan for developing a petroleum reservoir that is often based on reservoir simulation.

FFM (full-field model)

A reservoir model of an entire oil or gas reservoir. When computing capacity is limited, it is often necessary to build and process a sector model (or piece) of the entire reservoir model.

FAST (fracture-assisted steamflood technology)

A process for the recovery of heavy crude oil and bitumen patented by Continental Oil Company.

GIIP (gas initially in-place)

Volume of dry natural gas or gas condensate in-place at discovery.

HC (hydrocarbon)

Crude oil, natural gas or gas condensate.

HOP (heavy oil process)

A patented process for recovering heavy oil by injecting steam into horizontal wells drilled from a subterranean chamber excavated at the base of a vertical shaft.

HS (himself)

The author James Dietrich.

IPE (independent petroleum engineer)

A designation given to a third party charged with developing an unbiased estimate of the ownership share in a jointly owned oil reservoir.

J_D (dimensionless productivity index)

A technical term used to express the productive capacity of an oil well. The higher the J_D, the more productive the well.

KR (Kern River)

The Kern River heavy oil field located near Bakersfield, California is one of America's oldest and most prolific fields.

MWAG (miscible water and gas)

An enhanced oil recovery technology involving the injection of water and carbon-dioxide or enriched hydrocarbon gas to miscibly displace crude oil.

MO (Maersk Oil)

A privately owned international oil and gas company headquartered in Denmark that was sold to the French oil company Total in 2018.

N_{res} / G (net reservoir to gross ratio)

The fraction of a gross interval within a petroleum reservoir that stores hydrocarbons that will flow.

N_{rock} / G (net rock to gross ratio)

The fraction of a gross interval within a petroleum reservoir that stores hydrocarbons.

OOIP (oil originally in-place)

Volume of oil in-place at discovery.

OPC (Oilfield Production Consultants)

A consultancy located in London that seconds contract staff into clients' offices.

PA (production attainment)

The ratio of actual production to the production promised at project approval, an assurance often based on reservoir modeling.

Permeability

A measure of the ability of a rock to allow fluids to pass through it. Permeability is related to the shapes of the pores (or voids) in a rock and their level of connectedness.

Porosity

A measure of the void (or "empty") spaces in a rock that are filled by oil, water and/or gas. It is the fraction of the volume of voids over the total volume, varying between 0 and 1.

PWRI (produced water re-injection)

The technology involved in returning water produced with oil back into the subsurface.

Reservoir Model

A two or three-dimensional digital representation of a petroleum reservoir that is processed by a reservoir simulator.

Reservoir Simulator

A computer program that simulates the depletion history of a petroleum reservoir and forecasts its future behavior under alternative development and operating schemes.

SAGD (steam-assisted gravity drainage)

An enhanced oil recovery technology for producing heavy crude oil and bitumen.

SH (share holder)

A company or entity owning a fraction of a petroleum reservoir.

STEM (science, technology, engineering and mathematics)

A term used to group together these disciplines in education.

SUCO (Suez Oil Company)

A joint venture between the German company RWE Dea and the Egyptian General Petroleum Company in Egypt.

TCM (technical committee meeting)

Meetings, usually regularly scheduled, that are attended by technical representatives of a company or entity owning a fraction of a petroleum reservoir.

TDRM (top-down reservoir modeling)

A proprietary modeling technique developed by British Petroleum that involves the use of simple, coarse reservoir models.

TS (trailing spouse)

Mary Dietrich, spouse of the author.

WI (Wintershall)

Wintershall Holding GmbH, based in Kassel, is Germany's largest crude oil and natural gas producer. It is a wholly owned subsidiary of the German chemical company BASF.

Y-T (Yurubcheno-Tokhomskoye)

An oil and gas field in Eastern Siberia owned by the East Siberia Oil and Gas Company.